CONTENTS

JOURNEY TO *THE LAST JEDI*

How do you follow a critical and commercial smash hit like *Star Wars: The Force Awakens*? Rian Johnson and his team had a plan to take the story forward....

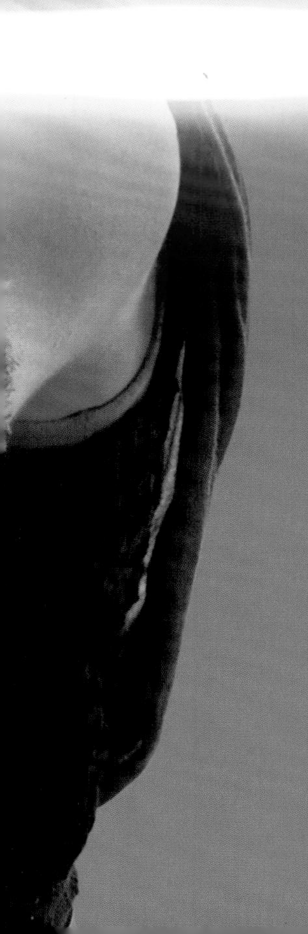

2 /

In the hands of director (and co-writer) J.J. Abrams, *The Force Awakens* (2015) opened an exciting new chapter in the sprawling saga of *Star Wars*. Now it would fall to another to continue that story—a writer/director whose idiosyncratic and varied filmography includes the neo-noir cult classic *Brick* (2005) and the mind-bending time traveling thriller *Looper* (2012): Rian Johnson.

For President of Lucasfilm Kathleen Kennedy, it was Johnson's unique and specific vision that made him the right person to take up the directing baton passed on by J.J. Abrams. In addition, Kennedy points to the fact that Johnson "writes amazingly fierce and independent women," and that the director "has a great sense of humor, which is so vital to the character of *Star Wars*.

"Rian observes human behavior really well," Kennedy says. "He's got a very good heart and a real soul to what he does. A filmmaker's particular style and vision is what shapes these stories, and that shines through in Rian's film."

For his part, Johnson freely admits that agreeing to come on board to write and direct *The Last Jedi* was a big decision, one that he took some time to think about. While on the one hand it was obviously a dream opportunity, on the other it was evident it would also be a life-changing episode, and Johnson was keen that it should be a good experience.

In any event, Johnson's decision to take up the challenge was vindicated by the incredible adventure the undertaking turned out to be. Like many his age, *Star Wars* had always been an intrinsic part of his life: "Some of my earliest memories of creative play, of telling my own stories, were with *Star Wars* toys and in that universe," he notes. Accordingly, Johnson had anticipated "much more fear and trepidation at the weight of actually working on a real *Star Wars* film." ►

3 /

4 /

1 / Rey as played by Daisy Ridley. (See previous page)

2 / Kelly Marie Tran and John Boyega work through the script with director/writer Rian Johnson.

3 / Rey becomes more attuned with the Force as Luke looks on. (See opposite page)

4 / Kylo Ren's rage gets the better of him as he becomes more conflicted over his true nature.

"I had the time of my life making this movie."

Rian Johnson

But while, inevitably, there was pressure and expectation, and attendant nerves and fear, Johnson felt that as a result of his "primal connection to the world, the overriding emotion of the process was happiness. I had the time of my life making this movie. In many ways it felt the closest I've ever gotten to a professional equivalent of that freewheeling play, being a kid and running around the room with action figures."

By far the biggest film that Johnson has made to date—in both size and scope—his attitude going in was to jump right in and tackle it headlong. "If I had let myself zoom back and look at the enormity of the task, and the responsibility of it, I would have just been paralyzed and spent the last few years curled up in the fetal position." Examining where *The Force Awakens* had left matters, Johnson wrote down the names of each of the characters and began asking himself what he knew about them. "What do I think they want? Where can I see them going? And what would be the hardest thing for each of them to come up against? And once I got to a place where I had something for each one of them that made sense, I started drawing it out into a story. So it's kind of like eating an elephant. You just do it one bite at a time."

Johnson knew that he didn't have to concentrate so much on the epic nature of the film, understanding that the bigger elements of the movie—the battles and general spectacle—would flow from simply getting to play within the *Star Wars* universe. Much more important were the characters and the story. Not only did these need to be the starting point for the whole enterprise, but with the film being the middle part of a trilogy, it was necessary to take some time to drill down into what made the characters tick.

5 /

6 /

5 / A porg (the brainchild of Rian Johnson) offers some comic relief.

6 / Finn embarks on a journey of discovery as he attempts to save the Resistance.

7 / While much of *The Force Awakens* was about the search for Luke Skywalker, *The Last Jedi* dealt with why he didn't want to be found.

"Rian was able to come up with a story that was powerful and emotional and goes in an unexpected way."

Ram Bergman

Ram Bergman, Johnson's longtime producing partner, notes that it's "always about the characters" for the director, and that by making them his starting point, "he was able to come up with a story that was powerful and emotional and goes in an unexpected way. The story is what is true for the characters; it takes them on a journey that feels real."

As alluded to by Kathleen Kennedy, a big part of the appeal of *The Last Jedi* for Johnson was the presence of strong female characters. "One of the first things that Kathy told me when she asked me if I'd be interested in doing this was that the lead character was a girl named Rey. I was instantly into that; it just felt right. Leia was the first female figure that girls and women could look up to, and seeing how much it meant to them, Carrie Fisher was very conscious of that and held that with her. She felt a responsibility to make Leia great."

But *The Last Jedi* offered the tantalizing prospect of introducing yet more compelling females to the *Star Wars* saga, as well as expanding on existing ones. Alongside Rey and Leia, there are new characters, such as Rose and Vice Admiral Holdo, and returning ones, such as Captain Phasma—a mix of, as Johnson puts it, "really interesting strong and powerful and weak and conflicted and good and bad female characters" —portrayed by an amazing array of acting talent. "There are a lot of kick-ass women in this movie," says Johnson, "which is pretty great."

One of the most vital aspects of the story was the relationship between Rey and Luke Skywalker; as such, this was something that Johnson needed to work out as a writer. When Rey arrives at the island on Ahch-To where Luke has retreated, she has her expectations of who and what the Jedi Master is, but Johnson needed to work out why Luke was on the island. "Because I know he's not a coward and I know he's not hiding. I know if he's there, he's taken himself out of the fight, and he must have a reason for doing that. What is that reason?"

Ultimately, the writer/director was able to get to a place where he could put himself in Luke's shoes, to understand who Luke is and how events had conspired to get Luke to the island. "Now, let's see what happens when Rey comes into his life and messes everything up, by showing up on his doorstep with a lightsaber," says Johnson.

8 /

8 / Phasma and her loyal stormtroopers.

9 / Poe Dameron and Vice Admiral Holdo clash as the Resistance's plight increases.

MAGICAL REALISM

Intrinsic to any *Star Wars* film is the contribution of Industrial Light & Magic (ILM), and *The Last Jedi* is no different. The team at ILM brought to bear the full might of their artistry and skills—in concert with the practical creatures and special effects—in order to help realize director Rian Johnson's vision.

For ILM visual effects supervisor Ben Morris, *Star Wars* is an indelible part of not just film history, but the wider popular culture, stretching from the 20th into the 21st century. As a consequence, the audience has a firm idea of what *Star Wars* is, so it was important for Morris to give that audience something they hadn't seen before, and yet still reference, as he puts it, the "visual languages and aesthetics and choreography and action that people respond to as being from the world of *Star Wars*." That process involved ILM "designing those ideas very early on in production so they can inform how we shoot with the real actors and the real sets."

Shot on anamorphic 35mm film, Arri Alexa and IMAX, *The Last Jedi* utilized real-world locations and practical sets whenever possible, lending the production a veracity that was difficult for ILM to replicate. But the team rose to the challenge, the authentic nature of the footage giving them a tangible realism on which to build the more than 2000 visual effects shots they created, whether it be digital set extensions or entirely digital locales.

9 /

1 /

RIAN JOHNSON
DIRECTOR ON SET

Go behind-the-scenes to see *Star Wars: The Last Jedi*'s visonary director Rian Johnson at work, and sometimes play...

2 /

1 / Offering some direction to Joonas Suotamo (Chewbacca). (See opposite page)

2 / Sharing a joke with John Boyega (Finn) and Oscar Isaac (Poe Dameron).

3 / A moment's contemplation with Carrie Fisher (General Organa).

4 / Lining up a shot with a tough-looking Daisy Ridley (Rey).

3 /

4 /

5 /

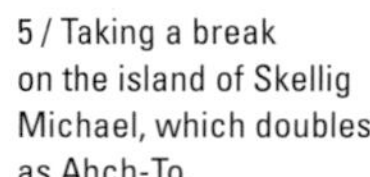

5 / Taking a break on the island of Skellig Michael, which doubles as Ahch-To.

6 / Johnson flanked by producers Ram Bergman and Kathleen Kennedy.

7 / Johnson and Bergman share a moment with Joonas Suotamo (Chewbacca). (See opposite page)

8 / The things we do for *Star Wars*! Johnson and the crew shoot on a waterlogged set. (See opposite page)

6 /

7 /

8 /

9 /

10 /

9 / Directing Carrie Fisher as Leia takes command of the *Raddus*.

10 / Bergman and Johnson relax on a Resistance transport.

11 / Johnson cheekily signs the *Millennium Falcon*, replacing the former and future *Star Wars* director JJ Abrams! (See opposite page)

12 / Photoreceptor level with BB-8. Jimmy Vee, the actor who plays R2-D2 in *The Last Jedi*, can been seen to the left of this shot. (See opposite page)

11 /

12 /

AHCH-TO

In a remote corner of the galaxy, a disillusioned Jedi Master is shocked to be confronted by a piece of his past.

REY

MAY THE FORCE BE WITH HER

The Force has awakened in Rey. But for her powers to be put at the service of the Resistance, she needs guidance.

Abandoned by her parents as a child, Rey lived alone on the desert planet of Jakku, waiting—hoping—for her family's eventual return. To survive in this harsh, unforgiving environment, she became a scavenger and a fighter, but each night she gazed up at the stars, longing for something more.

Rey's life radically changed when she encountered Finn, a fugitive stormtrooper on the run from the First Order, and BB-8, an astromech droid belonging to Resistance fighter Poe Dameron. Forming an alliance, Rey, Finn, and BB-8 fled an attack by the nefarious First Order, blasting away from Jakku aboard a starship they stole from a junkyard: the *Millennium Falcon*. Linking up with the ship's rightful owners, Han Solo and Chewbacca—former heroes of the Rebel Alliance against the Empire who had returned to a life of smuggling, they joined the Resistance against the First Order.

On the planet Takodana, Rey learned about the Force, a mystical, invisible energy that surrounds and penetrates all living things, binding the galaxy together. To her surprise, she discovered she had a strong connection to the Force, so strong that, on Starkiller Base —an entire planet converted into a superweapon by the First Order—she was able to hold her own against the powerful Kylo Ren in a lightsaber duel… and even best him.

Even so, Rey's nascent abilities could easily lead her to the dark side of the Force. Realizing that she needed the wisdom of a Jedi Master to guide her along the right path, Rey sought out the legendary Luke Skywalker. She found him on an island on the remote world of Ahch-To—a place familiar to her from visions she experienced whilst still on Jakku—but when she hands Luke his old lightsaber, the weapon built by his father Anakin Skywalker, alias Darth Vader, he rejects it. Moreover, when she asks him to help her and the Resistance, by rejoining their ranks and opposing the First Order, he refuses. As far as Luke is concerned, the Jedi must end.

As stubborn as she is tenacious, Rey doesn't relent—the stakes are far too high for her to give in now. Finally, with a little assistance from Luke's old astromech droid, R2-D2, she persuades the old master to teach her the ways of the Force.

Initially, Luke merely wants her to understand his reasons and then leave, but Rey proves to be of a different level from anyone else he has ever trained. Her mysterious bond to the dark side and to Kylo Ren is something Skywalker has never seen before —a, powerful and dangerous connection. But it's only through that bond that Rey will be able to understand who she really is.

2 /

3 /

4 /

1 / The mysterious Rey. (See previous page)

2 / Lightsaber ignited! Will Rey become a Jedi?

3 / Rey recovers from seeing an intense image in the Force.

4 / In training with her trusty staff on Ahch-To.

5 / Rey refuses to be defeated by Luke's apathy. (See opposite page)

6 /

6 / Rey takes the gunning station of the *Millennium Falcon* as the First Order closes in!

7VIV

THE APPRENTICE
DAISY RIDLEY

Despite her adventures, finding Luke Skywalker is only the start of a personal journey that leads Rey to confront her past.

DRESSED FOR THE WEATHER

While costume designer Michael Kaplan was keen that Rey's clothing should reflect the new environments she would be traveling to, he didn't want the change to be too drastic. "She's finding her inner strength," he explains, "but she's still Rey. Just enough of a change to move her, and her story, along." Having originally been dressed for the desert in *The Force Awakens*, it made sense that she would adopt a poncho now that she was heading for a place with cooler, rainier weather. "The colors have changed too for the same environmental reasons: while the pale colors worked on Jakku, darker colors seemed more appropriate for where she is going."

1 / Rey gets attuned to using the power of the Force — and a lightsaber! (See opposite page)

At the end of *The Force Awakens*, Rey's mission to find the reclusive Luke Skywalker reached its conclusion on the distant planet of Ahch-To. But for the young woman from the backwater desert world of Jakku—and for the actress who plays her, Daisy Ridley—the adventure was just beginning.

According to Ridley, finally getting to meet Luke—a legendary figure even on such an out-of-the-way place as Ahch-To—is an eye-opening experience for Rey. "I think she's learning not to believe the hype," says the actress. For the figure she finds before her is not everything she's been led to believe: "Good people make bad choices, and bad people can make good choices. She's learning her own strengths and weaknesses and continuing to learn about the human psyche, because she hasn't really had relationships with people before.

"Rey doesn't see herself as this powerful being," she continues, "and seeing Luke is a reflection of what people see her as. They talk about her potential, and she doesn't really feel it. But she does start to come around. She tries to move forward and do the right thing, like she has always done."

For director Rian Johnson, Rey's motivations were an important part of the story he was crafting. Noting that Rey had been thrown into a huge adventure in *The Force Awakens*, even before being dispatched by the Resistance to find Luke, Johnson points to Rey's desire for some kind of connection to her past, and her belief that there are answers out there somewhere. "I think she probably expects there are some answers about who she is, and that's really what she is on a quest to find out. Not just meaning who her parents are or where she comes from, but meaning what's her place in all of this? When she shows up on that island, there's part of her, and there's a big part of us, that expects that she's going to get that information from Luke."

Hailing Daisy Ridley as "an extraordinary young actor," Johnson highlights the incredible depth and emotion that she brought to the role of Rey. "I discovered that so much that people respond to in the character of Rey comes from Daisy: her tenacity, her bravery, her humor, her depth, so many things that make little kids want to be Rey, those things are Daisy."

It's an insight that is echoed by Ridley herself. "I like that I never questioned being a heroic woman in a film, and that's thanks to my upbringing. My mom's always worked; the women I grew up around always worked and were inspirational. So it's weird because the way people reacted made me question more than I did. It's a great role but not just because she's a woman. That's how simple it was to me. But others were like, 'This is a big deal,' clearly. It's exciting to be a part of that, and I'm thinking, *Let's continue. This is how it should be.*"

Ridley found working with both Mark Hamill and Adam Driver, who plays the First Order's Kylo Ren, a rewarding experience, albeit in very different ways. "Mark's a talker and Adam isn't," she says. "Mark has lived a crazy life. A lot of his life has been influenced by *Star Wars*, and he's so well-known for it. He's older; he's a father, so his energy is steadier. Adam is incredible. He has this amazing depth of emotion. I don't know anyone else like him. He's amazing to work with. He's a very generous actor."

As for the story Rian Johnson has crafted, Ridley highlights its unexpected nature, and the fact that each character is given the chance to progress. "And even though it's the second episode in this series, it is its own thing without just leading onto the next one, which is great."

LUKE SKYWALKER

BEYOND THE LAST HOPE

Choosing to go into exile after his dream of a new training school turns into a nightmare, Luke looks to be the last Jedi. Is this really the end of the order that once protected the galaxy?

For what seemed like an eternity to him, Luke Skywalker lived on the remote desert world of Tatooine with his Aunt Beru and Uncle Owen. A restless farm boy, Luke dreamed of a life of adventure—of being able to attend the Imperial Academy and becoming an ace pilot.

Luke had always been told by his uncle that his father, Anakin Skywalker, had been a navigator aboard a spice freighter. But the younger Skywalker's life changed forever when he learned that not only was Anakin in fact a Jedi Knight who fought in the Clone Wars, but also that he subsequently became Darth Vader, the Emperor's most feared and powerful emissary, and a champion of the dark side of the Force.

Events repeatedly brought Luke into conflict with his father. An encounter at Cloud City, high above Bespin, had Luke wielding Anakin's own lightsaber against him, but he ultimately lost it—along with his right hand. Later, at the climax of another epic duel, this time on a reconstituted Death Star, Luke resisted the lure of the dark side only to come under attack by the watching Emperor. Stricken at Luke's plight, Darth Vader repented, his compassion for his son ultimately defeating the Emperor—albeit at the cost of Vader's life—and saving the galaxy, restoring peace and freedom.

For many years thereafter, Luke chose not to take on an apprentice, until he came to realize just how powerful his nephew was. Ben Solo, the son of Han Solo and Luke's sister, Leia Organa, had the Skywalker blood flowing through his veins, and therefore had a natural affinity with the Force. Luke took Ben and a group of students and established a training temple, hoping to revive the defunct Jedi Order. But the darkness rising in Ben was uncontrollable, and led the young apprentice to commit a terrible act of betrayal. Ben destroyed the temple and killed his fellow students.

The balance between the light and the dark was shattered. Holding himself responsible for the tragedy, Luke attempted to bury the past—and the Jedi Order along with it—by vanishing. He headed for the remote world of Ahch-To, far from his sister Leia, who desperately needed him to join the fight against the First Order.

Electing to live a simple life, Luke follows a strict routine, from harvesting everything he needs from the island to taking shelter inside an ancient hut. It is a life of quiet solitude away from galactic conflict—until the fateful day the *Millennium Falcon* appeared on the horizon, and the past came calling in the form of his father's long lost lightsaber, offered to him by a young, Force-sensitive woman.

2 /

3 /

1 / Luke Skywalker, hero of the Rebellion and lost Jedi. (See previous page)

2 / Rey attempts to persuade the last Jedi to return. (See opposite page)

3 / Luke Skywalker is reunited with a piece of his past.

4 / Inside a mysterious tree, Luke consults with ancient Jedi texts.

4 /

5 /

6 /

5 / Jedi Master Luke Skywalker ponders the mysteries of Rey.

6 / Luke Skywalker, a Jedi in exile.

7 / The mythic Luke Skywalker.

THE RETURN OF A JEDI
MARK HAMILL

Once a young man craving adventure and excitement, Luke Skywalker's abandonment of the ways of the Force comes as a shock to Rey.

CLOTHES MAKE THE MASTER

When it came to dressing Mark Hamill's Luke Skywalker, costume designer Michael Kaplan felt that the grand robes Luke was seen in at the close of *The Force Awakens* wouldn't be appropriate for day-to-day life on Ahch-To. "While it was necessary that he starts *The Last Jedi* in the same costume, we very quickly see him going about his daily routines, and the robes would have been too cumbersome to navigate the rocky walkways. So we gave him some work clothes, a parka, and a backpack for supplies."

1 /

Returning to the iconic character that he first helped define 40 years ago, Mark Hamill notes that Luke Skywalker's state of mind at the beginning of *The Last Jedi*—a direct continuation of the end of *The Force Awakens*—is at first ambiguous. "Rey offers him the lightsaber, and he just stares at her."

For Rey, Luke is almost a mythological figure, something that impacts how she—indeed how everyone—perceives him. "At some point, people doubt he's a real person," says Hamill. "Because of the gravity of the situation, the urgency of the situation, she doesn't have the luxury of getting to know him and relax and exchange ideas. She needs him and wants to enlist his help and abilities to her cause. And that's the conflict. Luke's in a very different place than we've ever seen him before."

Where that place is, is a state of disillusionment. After tragedy struck his attempt to rebuild the Jedi Order, Luke Skywalker renounced the notion of the Jedi and took a long step back from galactic affairs. "Luke always represented hope and optimism," says Hamill. "And now, here he is pessimistic, disillusioned, and demoralized."

Despite initial reservations regarding Rian Johnson's plans for Luke, Hamill found working with the writer/director a positive experience, reporting that "There's no one more deserving of trust." It was Johnson's varied filmography that for Hamill was a big part of the appeal of working with the director. "If you look at his movies, each is different than the last. You can't pigeonhole him and say, 'That's the kind of film he makes.' That's what will happen with *The Last Jedi*. It's so different in many ways, subtle ways, than the other *Star Wars* movies, and yet it is satisfying in delivering what the fans want to see as well."

Something that was familiar for Hamill was stepping onto the *Millennium Falcon* set. Describing the experience as "bittersweet," he found memories came flooding back. "It's like going to your old high school or the house you lived in in sixth grade. The detail's perfect. It's just as I remember it. I climbed up and down the ladder, got in the hold where we stowed away, and sat in the cockpit with my grown children and wife. Later I slipped away and got really choked up. This is a moment, and it'll be gone."

1 / Rey watches as Luke performs his humble, if energetic, daily routine.

2 / Mark Hamill's powerful and thoughtful performance in the movie has won the actor much critical acclaim. (See opposite page)

THE ISLAND

An isolated environment, the island is the location of an ancient Jedi temple and a missing Jedi Master.

HEAD FOR HEIGHTS

While the formidable sea cliff at Sybil Head provided an ideal setting for the Jedi Village, it still required some digital enhancement to match Rian Johnson's vision. That required ILM visual effects supervisor Ben Morris to get airborne. "What I've had to do is go out in a helicopter and shoot plates that will allow us to extend the cliff to at least 1000 feet high," he reveals. "That's been good fun and we've been picking up some amazing sunsets as well."

1 /

Picking up directly where *The Force Awakens* ends, *The Last Jedi* begins on the remote world of Ahch-To, and the small island where Luke Skywalker has chosen to retreat from galactic affairs.

For director Rian Johnson, Skellig Michael, situated seven miles off the southwest coast of Ireland, offered the kind of "alien and unearthly" landscape that perfectly captured the sense that this was "a galaxy far, far away." But as fitting as the island was visually, practically it proved rather less so, especially for the length of time the crew would need to shoot there: not only was it inaccessible, it was also a nature reserve, home to a number of important seabird populations.

The production was faced with the task of finding a more feasible filming locale that still matched the grandeur and beauty of Skellig Michael, which had come to inform Johnson's vision of Ahch-To. Fortunately, Sybil Head, on Ireland's west coast and within eyesight of Skellig Michael, provided the solution. Featuring a landscape with the same structure as the island, along with dramatic cliffs, and an orientation to the sun that allowed the unit to shoot within the set while being able to see how precariously located in the environment it was, it even boasted an ocean view.

Not that this meant it didn't present challenges of its own. Besides the Jedi Village—a cantilevered set perched atop a 600-foot cliff, comprising beehive-shaped huts shipped over from Pinewood Studios and reconstructed—the team had to create the roads, facilities, and infrastructure needed to bring the huge crew to the remote location. That they managed it is still a source of amazement to Rian Johnson, who also praises "the tremendous local craftsmen who worked alongside our crew to give us this visceral experience not only for us but ultimately for the audiences."

According to supervising art director Chris Lowe, the wonder expressed by Johnson was echoed by the rest of the cast and crew: "The look on everyone's face when we walked onto the set on the edge of a cliff on that first bright May morning was jaw-dropping." Hailing the audacity of the decision to place the huts on the side of a mountain, Lowe has no doubt that the end results prove it was worth it: "Filmically it's one of the best things I've ever done."

And Sybil Head was just one of the places the production ventured to on the Wild Atlantic Way. Over a two-week period, the unit shot at four other locations, from its northern tip at Malin Head to its southern end at Mizen Head, and at Brow Head and Loop Head along the way.

1 / A docile thala-siren enjoys a nice rest on the rocks!

2 / The stunning scenery of Skellig Michael makes for a mysterious setting for Luke's exile. (See opposite page)

LANAIS

More intelligent than their distant evolutionary cousins, the porgs, the Lanais are native to Ahch-To and have been maintaining the island for generations.

CUTE CRITTERS

Sweet little creatures that observe the drama on the island, porgs are miniature masters of mischief.

PORG LIFE

By necessity, evolution on Ahch-To has led to species that live in the island to be water-based or at least amphibious. The bird-like porgs gain their sustenance from the sea, feasting on fish that they share with their porglets."

1 /

1 / A bunch of porgs huddle together.

2 / A curious pair of porgs take in the drama unfolding on Ahch-To. (See opposite page)

Among the many new creatures created *The Last Jedi*, the porgs—a species native to Ahch-To that resembles a cross between a puffin, an owl and a baby seal—have proved one of the more popular, both with fans and with the crew on set. According to creature designer Neal Scanlan, he and his team were pointed toward puffins by Rian Johnson as a basis for the porgs. "But as we learned more about the film and found out that they have specific moments, it very much informed the process. The design has to be a certain way, otherwise it won't have the ability to communicate or emote. So it leads you in that direction."

Scanlan's team built and performed an impressive array of different porg puppets throughout the shoot, from which the cameras garnered many practical shots, but during postproduction the filmmakers decided to extend some of the comedy and performances featuring the porgs. This entailed ILM building perfectly matching CG versions of the characters, allowing them to create a broader and often more complex range of movement as required. Taking care to match the real feathers on the puppets, ILM groomed thousands of corresponding CG feathers and soft facial fur onto the porgs. The result was an approximately 50/50 split of practical and CG porgs in the film, often having both techniques seamlessly integrated into the same shot.

CHEWBACCA
THE HEART OF A WARRIOR

With Han Solo gone, the first mate of the *Millennium Falcon* is missing a captain—someone he can both depend on and take care of.

A wise and seasoned operator—despite initial appearances to the contrary—the Wookiee Chewbacca has fought and survived many battles. During the Clone Wars, in a time before the Empire asserted its dark dominion over the galaxy, Chewbacca served as a combat engineer on his home planet of Kashyyyk, fighting alongside Jedi Master Yoda and the Grand Army of the Republic against the unrelenting forces of the Separatists' battle droids.

Later, together with inveterate rogue Han Solo, he became a smuggler and a pirate. As the first mate and the captain of the *Millennium Falcon*—a heavily modified Corellian freighter—Chewie and Han traversed the galaxy trading stolen cargo in the service of assorted interplanetary crime lords, among them the repulsive and dangerous Jabba the Hutt.

It is during this time that Chewie, along with Han, encountered a young farm boy named Luke Skywalker on the desert planet Tatooine. Joining the reclusive Jedi Master Obi-Wan Kenobi, the pair helped Luke rescue Princess Leia Organa of Alderaan from the clutches of the Imperials. Liberating her from deep within a monstrous, moon-sized weapon known as the Death Star, these unlikely compatriots subsequently assisted the Rebel Alliance in destroying the battle station. Han and Chewbacca later played a key role in taking down the Empire's more powerful second Death Star.

Some years later, when the *Millennium Falcon* was stolen, Chewie and Han searched the galaxy for their missing ship, scouring every system in an effort to locate their vessel. When they finally tracked it down, they were both are surprised to find it piloted by Rey, a woman who recently had fled the remote desert world Jakku. Agreeing to take Rey, her ally Finn, and their droid BB-8 to find the Resistance and General Organa, Chewbacca and Han wound up getting sucked into the conflict between the Resistance and the First Order. During a mission to the Starkiller Base to destroy the enemy's superweapon, Chewie lost his best friend when Han was killed at the hands of his estranged son, Kylo Ren.

For the first time in his life, the Wookiee found himself alone inside the cockpit of the *Millennium Falcon*. But his enforced solitude wasn't to last. Though Han was gone, there was still someone Chewie could help and protect—someone with an incredible talent for piloting; an individual to whom Han himself once offered a job: Rey.

Once again a first mate and copilot—roles he prefers—Chewbacca agreed to let the young scavenger fly the legendary spacecraft. Following a map, they went to the distant planet Ahch-To, where they found the self-exiled Luke Skywalker. While Rey tries to persuade Luke to teach her the ways of the Force, Chewie sticks close to the *Falcon*, waiting to see what transpires.

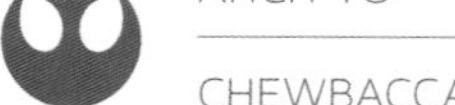

2 /

3 /

4 /

1 / The mighty Chewbacca roars into action! (See previous page)

2 / Chewie and Rey take control of the *Millennium Falcon.*

3 / A cute passenger joins Chewbacca in the *Falcon's* cockpit.

4 / The *Millennium Falcon* in the heat of battle.

FURRY FURY

JOONAS SUOTAMO

Faithful first mate and co-pilot Chewbacca now stands by Rey's side and accompanies her as she searches for Luke Skywalker.

When Finnish actor Joonas Suotamo stepped into Peter Mayhew's shoes to play Chewbacca, he found they were very big shoes—but he was up for the challenge. "You must interpret the role your own way," he says. "But I think we did a good job, everyone involved, in making the suit the best it could be, and I tried to do the best I could to be true to the character's past history and brought in new things when appropriate."

The former basketball-player-turned-actor adds, "I am a very happy person whenever I'm in the costume. When everyone sees Chewie, they don't see me, they see Chewie. And that means I did my job inside the suit. I wanted to give people a glimpse of what they had seen of Chewie before. That was my goal."

THE *MILLENNIUM FALCON*

The flagship of the original *Star Wars* trilogy returns once again! This time, Rey and Chewbacca fly the vessel to Ahch-To, hoping to bring Luke Skywalker back to the fight...

An iconic image of the fight against evil, the *Millennium Falcon* is now back in the hands of the Resistance after tumultuous years of being traded. A freighter, previously used by Han Solo and Chewbacca to smuggle for Jabba the Hutt, the impressive speed and maneuverability of the old ship is invaluable in the fight against the First Order. While on Ahch-To, Chewbacca carries out some much-needed maintenance on the *Falcon*, while being constantly interrupted by the mischievous porgs.

YT-1300F LIGHT FREIGHTER (MODIFIED)

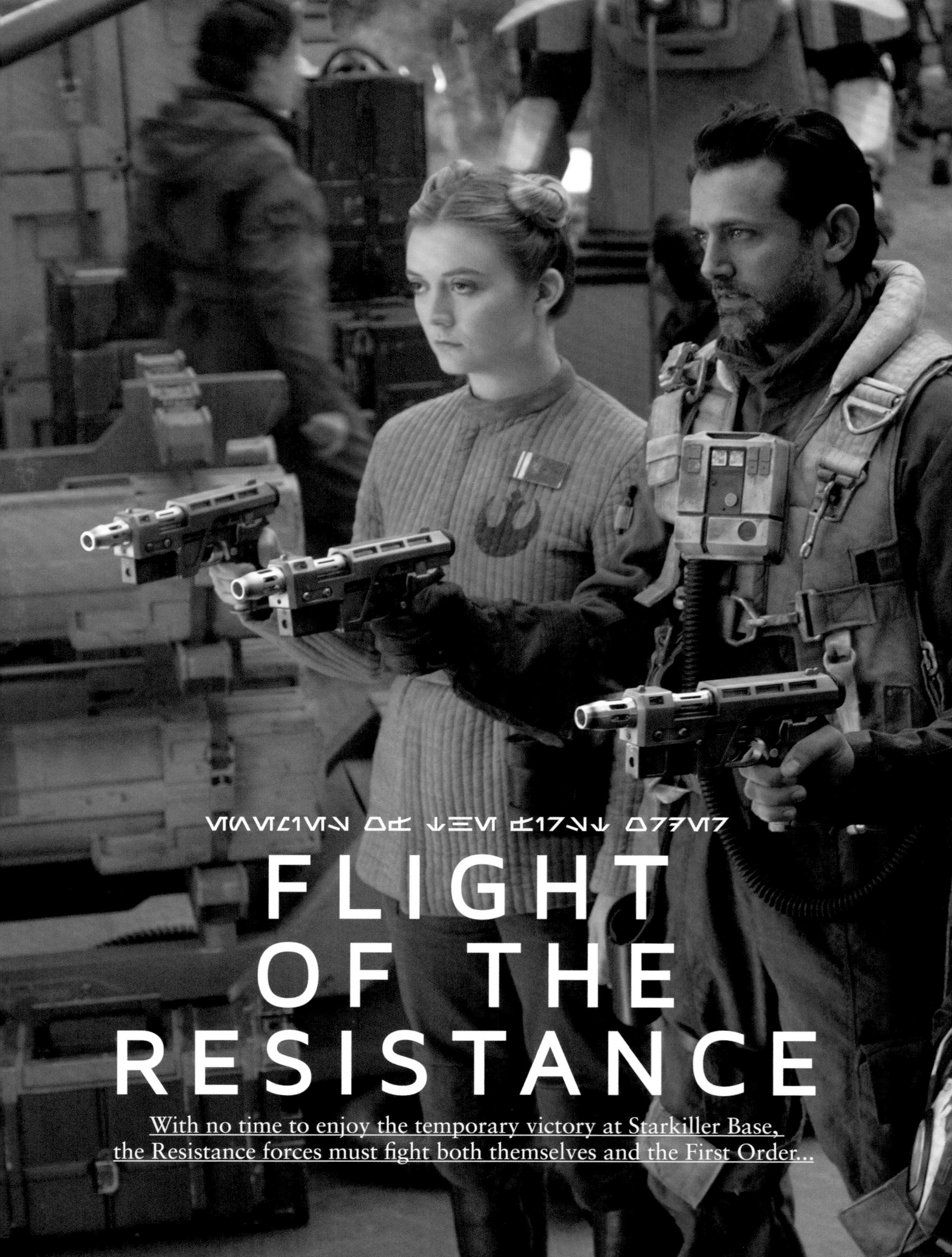

FLIGHT OF THE RESISTANCE

With no time to enjoy the temporary victory at Starkiller Base, the Resistance forces must fight both themselves and the First Order...

LEIA
LIGHTING THE WAY

In their most desperate hour, the members of the Resistance look to the princess who once defeated an Empire: Leia Organa.

The daughter of Senator Padmé Amidala and Jedi Knight Anakin Skywalker, as a baby Leia was adopted by the Royal Family of the planet Alderaan. Years later, when she found herself at the mercy of the notorious Darth Vader—her father's new identity—neither of them recognized the other.

However, the Skywalker blood runs in her veins, and though Leia has never been trained as a Jedi, the Force is strong with her. Rescued by Luke Skywalker, Han Solo, and Chewbacca from captivity aboard the Death Star, Princess Leia brought the plans for the Imperial superweapon to her fellow rebels on Yavin 4. A review of the Death Star's technical readout revealed a flaw that the rebels exploited to great success, destroying the battlestation.

Thereafter, elevated to the position of one of the most influential leaders in the Alliance, Leia was also part of the team that played a crucial role in the destruction of the second Death Star, and the end of the Empire.

Years later, Leia was the first to warn the senate about the danger posed by the First Order's activities. When her entreaties to the senators to put a stop to Snoke's arms race fell on deaf ears, Leia formed the Resistance in order to oppose the First Order.

General Organa knows that the Resistance is the galaxy's only hope of restoring peace and freedom, but in order for the movement to survive, a new generation of heroes must take her place. Preparing them for that task is Leia's paramount duty.

2 /

3 /

1 / Respected leader General Leia Organa. (See previous page)

2 / General Organa takes command of the *Raddus* as she attempts to lead the Resistance out of danger.

3 / Through connection of Force and blood, Leia can sense the dark presence of her son leading an attack on the Resistance fleet.

4 / The weight of responsibilty for the fleet weighs heavy on the general. (See opposite page)

LEADING THE WAY
CARRIE FISHER

An experienced commander, Leia faces her greatest struggle as the First Order closes in on the imperilled Resistance.

CARRIE FISHER ON *STAR WARS*

"For me, it's about family. That's what is so powerful about it. I go to Comic-Con and meet a lot of these people and it's very powerful for them. They're showing the films to their children and their grandchildren. They're sharing something that moved them as a child. That's personal. I've watched a lot of that over the years, like people coming in with babies that have the Princess Leia outfit on. That's the thing that makes it so powerful for a lot of people. It's an identifying universe and something that creates a community. Anything that does that can heal people. You can have that thing in common and find others. I don't know that it saves lives, but I know it improves them."

1 /

1 / Despite friction, Leia shares a bond with Poe Dameron.

2 / Carrie Fisher as General Leia. (See opposite page)

When Carrie Fisher tragically passed away in December 2016, Leia Organa's story in *The Last Jedi* was lent an added poignancy. Still leading the Resistance, Leia, the general and rebel princess, had been central to the *Star Wars* universe from its inception, and Fisher's passing was keenly felt by all concerned, not least producer Ram Bergman. "Carrie had a meaningful role in the film even before her untimely death," he says, "but now there is so much more weight to some very emotional scenes. She challenged Rian every day, but they had a great partnership. Everyone will be so proud of her performance."

Interviewed during production, Fisher said that she found her character in a different state this time around. As Fisher saw it, Leia had gone "from being someone who's shooting guns and swinging across chasms to killing Jabba the Hutt, to being serious, worrying a lot." As a result, the general is tired. "She has a lot more responsibility and there's a lot more reason for her to be exhausted."

One highlight for both Fisher and her character was getting to see Mark Hamill as Luke Skywalker once more. Fisher admitted that she always thought of Hamill as Luke, and that she and Hamill had a relationship that was akin to that of siblings. "Our relationships in the movie are very much like our relationships in life," she said. "We take care of each other, in a way."

As for Leia's relationship with ace Resistance pilot Poe Dameron, as portrayed by Oscar Isaac, that brought to mind a different dynamic. "Poe is Leia's protégé, and in a way she thinks of him as Han, which is both the good news and the bad news," she explained. "He's dominating and he doesn't listen to her. She's trying to train him. We have some moments together."

POE DAMERON

THE FUTURE IN HIS HANDS

Commander Poe Dameron is the best pilot in the Resistance—but in its darkest hour, he must become far more than that.

General Organa has always trusted Poe Dameron. Mission after mission Leia has heaped greater and greater responsibility on his shoulders. Of all the Resistance's operatives, it is Poe she entrusts with the most dangerous assignments, notably when she sent him to Jakku to retrieve the map to Luke Skywalker's location.

Aboard his distinctive black X-wing, Poe led a squadron of Resistance starfighters against the First Order, first on planet Takodana, then on Starkiller Base. His blasts started a chain reaction that ultimately led to the destruction of the ice planet.

When the First Order fleet intercepts the Resistance in the middle of the evacuation of D'Qar, Poe doesn't hesitate: following his instincts, he approaches the enemy's Dreadnought alone, aboard his light fighter, and takes out all its cannons before they realize he's merely a decoy. It's thanks to him that the bombers can start their attack in order to buy time for the evacuation to be completed.

However, Poe also has a reckless side. When General Organa orders him to disengage, Poe switches off the comm, hoping that the bombers will take down the Dreadnought. Which they do—but at a high cost… almost too high.

For his flagrant disregard of a direct order, Leia demotes him. She knows that Poe Dameron represents the future of the Resistance, but in order for him to become one of its more important members, he has to learn a vital lesson: that he cannot solve everything by jumping in his X-wing and blowing stuff up. He must learn patience and strategy; he must learn to think like a leader.

1 / Poe Dameron: Hero of the Resistance. (See previous page)

2 / Poe contemplates the future of the Resistance, as dark forces gather.

3 / Leading members of the Resistance in an act of defiance against Vice Admiral Holdo.

4 / Always on the move! Dameron races into action. (See opposite page)

2 /

4 /

3 /

REBEL, REBEL
OSCAR ISAAC

A pilot who flies on instinct, Poe Dameron's actions cause trouble for both the First Order and the Resistance!

1 /

ALL THAT JAZZ

Ruminating on his experience working with writer/director Rian Johnson, Oscar Isaac conjures an intriguing analogy. "Working with Rian reminds me of a West Coast jazz musician, giving a little direction here and there," he says. "He's very laid back, but very sharp. He knows his scale. He knows what he's playing. And he's open. He's open to trying things. He's willing to explore scenes with me, and often we end up going back to what the script says, but at least we get to explore."

For his part, Johnson sees Isaac as "a reincarnation of my favorite old movie stars; he has that old school magnetism paired with insane acting chops. Poe is a straight-up, good-guy hero, and although he gets put through the wringer in this film, because of Oscar you never lose faith that he's going to come out the other end all the better for it."

For Oscar Isaac, the contrast between his character in *The Force Awakens* and the Poe Dameron we find in *The Last Jedi* is appreciable, not least because we get to see more of Poe in the new film. Noting that in *The Force Awakens* Poe was "a man on a mission"—that mission being to find the missing Luke Skywalker—and that when Poe and Finn met the two characters sparked, Isaac maintains that we didn't learn much more than that about his character, "except that he has a smart mouth." In *The Last Jedi*, however, "there's a lot more conflict. He finds himself in a more precarious situation. He's a man of action; he wants to help, to save the Resistance, to fight the First Order. But his old heroics aren't necessarily what they need in this moment."

Like all of the characters in *The Last Jedi*, Poe is given room to grow and develop over the course of the film. In his case, that means "learning to not just be a soldier but to be a leader. Not just be the heroic pilot but perhaps learn to be a general. And that's a shift. He's a man on a mission. You give him a mission, and he'll complete it. But seeing the bigger picture, knowing when not to engage, that's what he has to learn."

It's a steep learning curve, and one that takes both Isaac's character, and the film in general, in a bold new direction. According to Isaac, *The Last Jedi* explores themes of "what it means to resist and what it means to win," and contains "some very truthful messages about power and the nature of power and those seeking power and how easily it can go one way or another."

He adds, "It's finding out what a hero is. What it is to be a hero and what it is to be a leader. You get more specific and find the nuance in the situation, and how you can explore those themes. It's a war. They're in the midst of a war; it is life and death, and the decisions made affect so many. Especially on Poe's side, which is focused on the Resistance."

1 / Poe Dameron has the First Order in his sights.

2 / Oscar Isaac as the rebellious Poe Dameron. (See opposite page)

AMILYN HOLDO
THE VICE ADMIRAL

A member of the Resistance and a longstanding friend of General Organa, Vice Admiral Holdo takes command at a critical time for the Resistance.

With her striking dyed hair and glamorous attire, Vice Admiral Amilyn Holdo doesn't look like a typical high-ranking officer. However, her military experience dates back to her time serving the Rebel Alliance in the early days of the Galactic Civil War.

Born on the planet Gatalenta, as a teenager Amilyn Holdo joined a political organization called the Apprentice Legislature, on Coruscant. During her time there, she met Princess Leia Organa of Alderaan and the two became friends, spending a great deal of time together attending senatorial sessions and routine pathfinding training on various worlds. Whilst on one such trip, Holdo learned of her friend's involvement with the Rebellion against the Galactic Empire. Soon after, Holdo helped Organa navigate safe passage to the Paucris system so that the princess could warn the rebel fleet that the Empire was poised to attack.

Later, after the Rebellion formally became the Alliance to Restore the Republic, and after a long fight to topple the evil dictator Palpatine during the subsequent Galactic Civil War, the Empire was finally defeated. The Alliance rebranded itself as the New Republic. But out of the ashes of the Imperial machine came a remnant reorganized into the First Order. Organa created the Resistance to oppose the First Order, with Holdo joining the cause some years later as a Vice Admiral.

When General Organa is injured as the Resistance flees the First Order, Holdo assumes command. However, while she is more than capable for the role, a number of Resistance members, chiefly Poe Dameron, bristle under her command, and are highly suspicious of her evasive manner.

THE ADMIRABLE VICE ADMIRAL

LAURA DERN

A commanding presence, Vice Admiral Amilyn Holdo's leadership is called into question when she replaces a stricken Leia.

A GALACTIC GOWN

In designing Vice Admiral Holdo's look, costume designer Michael Kaplan and his team began with a sketch of the character in a Resistance uniform, but director Rian Johnson was looking for something different. "He wanted her to be more independently dressed," says Kaplan, "balladic was the word he used, to show off her body, something she could be flirtatious in. A gown but one that had authority and presence." Highlighting Dern's "amazing posture," Kaplan notes that the acclaimed actress was "a dream to dress."

1 /

1 / Holdo takes aim as she fights for the survival of the Resistance.

2 / Laura Dern as Vice Admiral Amilyn Holdo. (See opposite page)

When Laura Dern signed on for *The Last Jedi*, the star of such unforgettable films as *Blue Velvet* (1986), *Wild at Heart* (1990) and *Jurassic Park* (1993) didn't really consider how iconic her character, Vice Admiral Holdo, might become. It was only when she heard someone asking how Holdo's hair color would work on a doll that she realized she was "serving something greater, as my childhood was served. You're not only serving storytelling but iconic and archetypal characters. I think about my daughter being a 10-year-old girl and the idea that she's going to have heroines in this story who all look very different and have very different qualities and natures, and are all fierce."

Dern enjoyed working with Rian Johnson, expressing her amazement that the director brought a process to *The Last Jedi* that for her brought to mind her experiences making independent films. "I've spent my life having different experiences and have been very fortunate to work with directors who want to mine the material and find more."

The actress has nothing but praise for the level of craft and attention to detail that went into *The Last Jedi*. "The word iconic is used correctly," says Dern. "I'm staring at iconic, archetypal characters and creatures and images from my own childhood. And I was in awe as everyone else when I walked on set."

DROIDS
A FORCE TO BE RECKONED WITH

More than merely machines providing technical support and assistance, these droids have proved to be an essential part of the Resistance.

BB-8

An unassuming spherical astromech droid, BB-8 has a particular aptitude for adventure. Prior to the destruction of Starkiller Base, BB-8 joined Poe Dameron on his mission to Jakku to retrieve information vital to the whereabouts of Luke Skywalker. When the droid and Poe were forced to separate, BB-8 was entrusted with the data. Employing all his ingenuity he managed to roll away from the stormtroopers searching for him and persuaded a young woman, Rey, to help him get off the planet and back to the Resistance.

After Rey leaves for Ahch-To with R2-D2 and Chewbacca, BB-8 aids Poe Dameron in the fight against the First Order Dreadnought during the evacuation of D'Qar. Ready and willing to risk everything for the Resistance, he's determined to accompany Finn and Rose on their sabotage mission aboard the enemy's flagship. He may not have been terribly enamored of Finn at first, but BB-8 now completely trusts the former stormtrooper.

R2-D2

Long before the demise of the Galactic Republic and the rise of the Empire, R2 was already a firmly established hero. Among his many feats of courage, he repaired the Naboo Royal Starship during an invasion, helping save Queen Amidala, the future mother of Luke and Leia.

When the Empire achieved dominance over the galaxy, R2 was serving Alderaan's royal family. Pursued by Darth Vader, Leia sent the droid on a desperate mission to Tatooine, where he met Luke. Along with Luke and protocol droid C-3PO, R2 played a vital role in the events that led to the end of the Empire and a return to galactic peace.

For years thereafter, the little droid and his master Luke stuck together—until Kylo Ren destroyed everything that Luke was trying to build. When the devastated Jedi went into self-imposed exile, R2 put himself into stand-by mode, only reactivating when the other portion of the map to Luke's location was revealed. Standing by Rey's side, R2 voyaged aboard the *Millennium Falcon* to Ahch-To, where he eagerly awaits a reunion with his master.

C-3PO

As a protocol droid, C-3PO is programmed to translate alien and cyborg languages or provide valuable information about customs and etiquette—not especially useful during, say, an evacuation or escape. Nonetheless, C-3PO—who's been with R2 since the beginning—does his best to help General Leia and the Resistance leaders find a way to move the fleet out of reach of the First Order.

2 /

3 /

4 /

1 / Resistance heroes C-3PO, R2-D2, and BB-8. (See previous page)

2 / BB-8 inside Poe's X-wing making repairs during a battle against the First Order.

3 / R2 aboard the ***Millennium Falcon***.

4 / C-3PO joins the Resistance's stand on Crait. (See opposite page)

DROID STORY
ANTHONY DANIELS

C-3PO's timid nature is ill-suited to being in the firing line of the First Order quite so often.

1 /

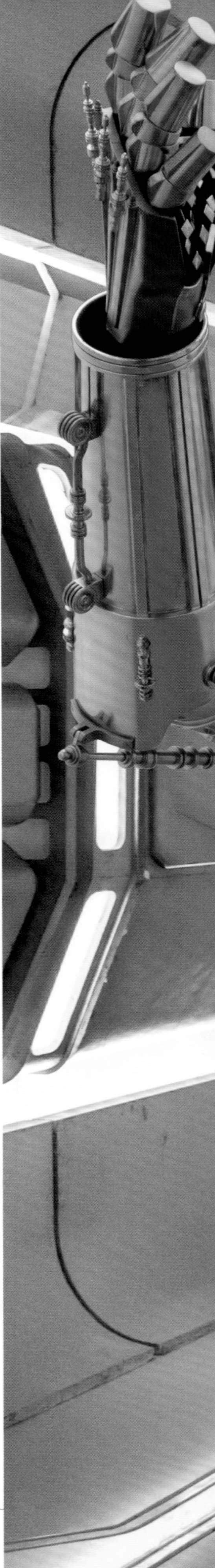

No *Star Wars* film would be complete without an appearance from C-3PO, and *The Last Jedi* is no different, as Anthony Daniels returns once more to portray the iconic droid. A constant voice of reason throughout the *Star Wars* saga—albeit one that isn't necessarily listened to—according to Daniels C-3PO's role is to act "as a little foil to all the drama that happens," as well as to offer some humanity—"which strangely enough coming out of a metal character, speaks louder than if a human character in the film said it."

Having been in every *Star Wars* film since the saga began in 1977, Daniels had no hesitations about donning the droid costume once again. For the actor, the adoration of the fans for the character and the franchise makes playing C-3PO worthwhile: "It makes me feel good when people come up and say, 'Thank you for my childhood.' That I'm a part of something they experienced as a kid and it's stayed with them for whatever reason. Nothing to do with me, mostly to do with George's bedrock story. But I now get that phrase: 'Thank you for my childhood.' It's something people carry with them now, forever. And now it's being passed on. Three generations get it."

1 / The ever-loyal C-3PO in the thick of the action!

2 / The protocol droid in a panic! (See opposite page)

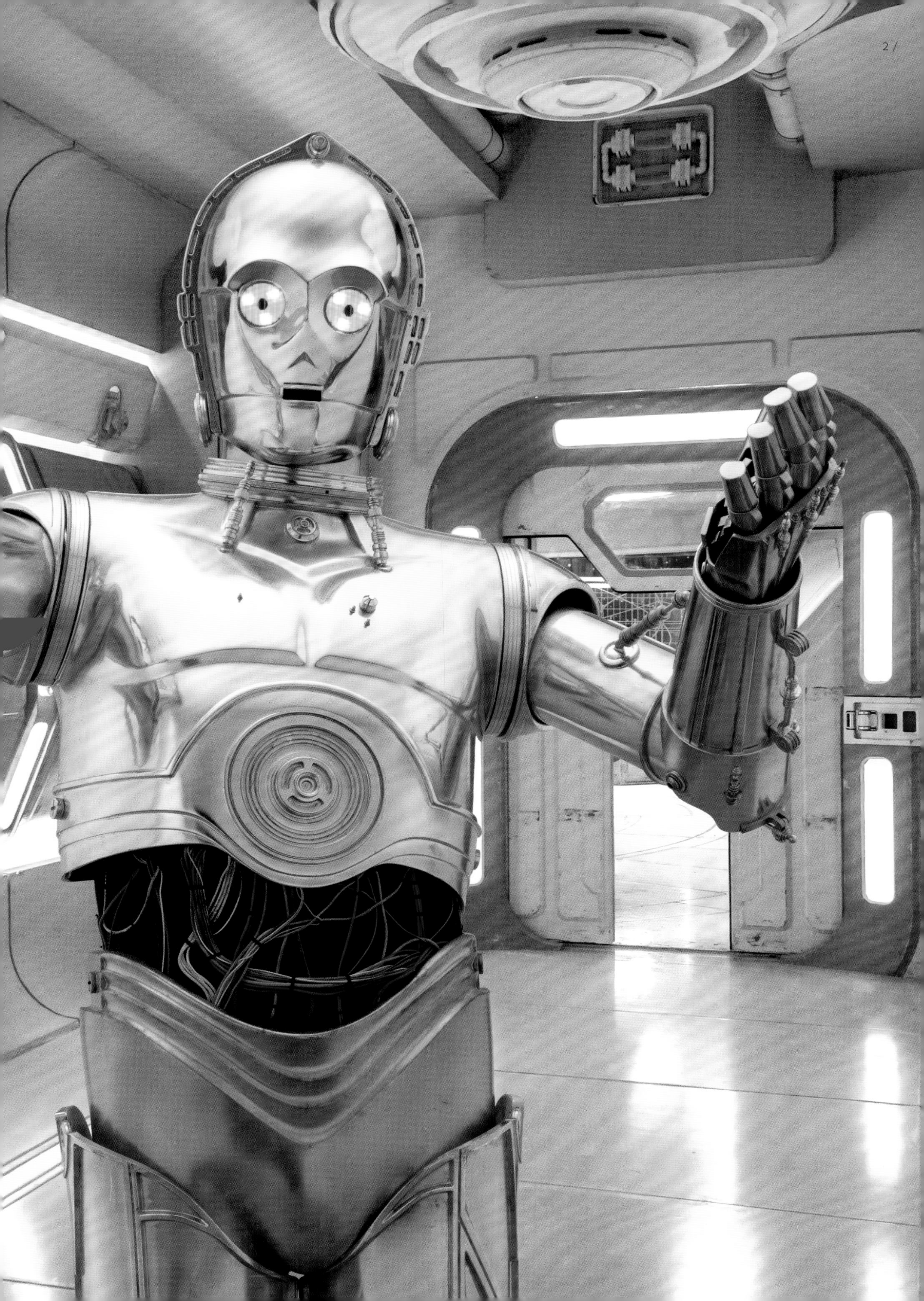

3 /

3 / C-3PO and R2-D2 are reunited aboard the *Millennium Falcon.*

RESISTANCE HIGH COMMAND

FIGHTING ON THE RUN

When Leia first formed the Resistance, many heeded her call. These courageous individuals hail from an array of backgrounds—from the Rebel Alliance, from independent defense forces, and from the New Republic.

1 /

2 /

COMMANDER D'ACY

In charge of the *Raddus*' bridge crew, and personally recruited by General Leia Organa herself, Larma D'Acy hails from the Warlentta system—a region which maintained its independence after the end of the Empire and refused to join the New Republic. Her family is responsible for protecting the sovereign space of their homeworld and welcomes her decision to join the Resistance.

3 /

LIEUTENANT CONNIX

Kaydel Connix serves as an operations controller on D'Qar. During the attack on Starkiller Base, her outstanding efforts to coordinate communications with Poe Dameron's squadron marked her out from the crowd. Promoted to lieutenant, she successfully leads the planet evacuation. Once the base is fully evacuated, Connix joins the *Raddus*' crew under the command of Admiral Ackbar and supreme commander General Organa.

1 / An emergency briefing aboard the *Raddus*.(See previous page)

2 / Resistance bridge Commander Larma D'Acy. (See previous page)

3 / Lieutenant Kaydel Connix.

4 / The Resistance face the wrath of the First Order!

4 /

5 /

5 / Admiral Ackbar takes command aboard the *Raddus*.

V-4X-D SKI SPEEDER

Obsolete vehicles which predate even the Rebellion era, these ultra-light, low altitude crafts, also known as skim speeders, are used during the Resistance's defence on Crait.

AN ARSENAL OF FREEDOM

The Resistance's efforts against the First Order's impressive fleet may seem to be hopeless, but they have a few ships that might just hold back their foe's attack.

T-70 X-WING

Perhaps the most easily identifiable starfighter in the Resistance's fleet, and the most advanced after the updated T-85s were understood to have all been destroyed in the Starkiller Base's attack on the Hosnian system.

RZ-2 A-WING INTERCEPTOR

Fast and maneuverable, the A-wing served the Rebel Alliance in the Galactic Civil War, and has been modified with refined cannon mountings, streamlining, and improvements to the jammers, making the craft far harder for enemies to target.

MILLENNIUM FALCON

Modified by its former owner, the late Han Solo, and his first mate, Chewbacca, into a speedier vessel, the *Falcon* is still a formidable ship despite its considerable age.

MG-100 STARFORTRESS

A bomber that was first used during the Galactic Civil War, this craft saw active service in peacetime when it was modified to perform cargo drops, wildfire suppression, and deploy explosives for mining.

THE GAMBLE

The place where the wealthy and corrupt of the galaxy come to play, Canto Bight's glamorous visage hides a darker, altogether more sinister underbelly.

As *The Last Jedi* production designer Rick Heinrichs points out, the franchise has frequently made use of otherworldly natural locations on Earth as stand-ins for planets in a galaxy far, far away; but it's rare for a *Star Wars* production to film in an urban environment. Daring to go to the kinds of places previous *Star Wars* films have seldom trod, for 10 days in March 2016 a splinter unit from *The Last Jedi* made their base in the medieval city of Dubrovnik—a UNESCO World Heritage Site that would double as the casino city Canto Bight.

Situated on the Dalmatian coast in southern Croatia, overlooking the Adriatic Sea, this Pearl of the Adriatic as it's known is arguably one of the world's most magnificent walled cities. As such, it presented quite a challenge for Heinrichs and the rest of the crew, both in terms of design and concept. "I was unsure how we'd take a real environment with architecture that has a familiarity about it and turn that into something that is part of the *Star Wars* galaxy," says the production designer.

Meeting these challenges certainly paid off, Dubrovnik's polished streets, swooping fortress walls and narrow alleyways offering all the romance that the filmmakers desired for Finn and Rose Tico's exotic adventure. Particularly impressive was the reflective quality of the streets, which were built with stacked and dressed stone, and the way the light was bouncing off of everything—a boon for director of photography Steve Yedlin, who made full use of the environment to create a unique and innovative look of the sequence.

1 /

CANTO BIGHT
WHERE THE WEALTHY RULE

On a planet far from the chaos, conflict, and suffering they helped cause, war profiteers reap the benefits of their amoral ways.

There's no place in the galaxy quite like the resort city of Canto Bight on planet Cantonica—a haven for those shady individuals making their fortunes by entering into contracts with the First Order, supplying its armories, or selling weapons, ammunition, and technology to independent groups preparing for a galactic war. In Canto Bight, local law enforcement is in the palm of the hand of the city's wealthy denizens, constantly patrolling the resort's streets, artificial coastline, and the Canto Casino and Racetrack.

This celebrated exclusive club—which boasts luxurious restaurants, a deluxe hotel, a shopping concourse, game rooms, and a fathiers racetrack—is where the galaxy's elite spends its wealth, taking chances at games like Savareen Whist, Zinbiddle, Uvide, and Hazard Toss (the clientele's favorite dice game). Only politicians, celebrities, and business magnates can afford these expensive pleasures—but spies and master codebreakers can hide themselves among them...

1 /

1 / Thamm, the best croupier in the business!

2 / Snook Uccorfay with Derla Pidys. (See opposite page)

3 / Assorted gamblers try their luck at the casino's tables.

4 / Performance artists Rhomby and Parallela Grammus.

5 / The mysterious, alluring "Lovey."

6 / The Contessa Alissyndrex delga Cantonica Provincion.

3 /

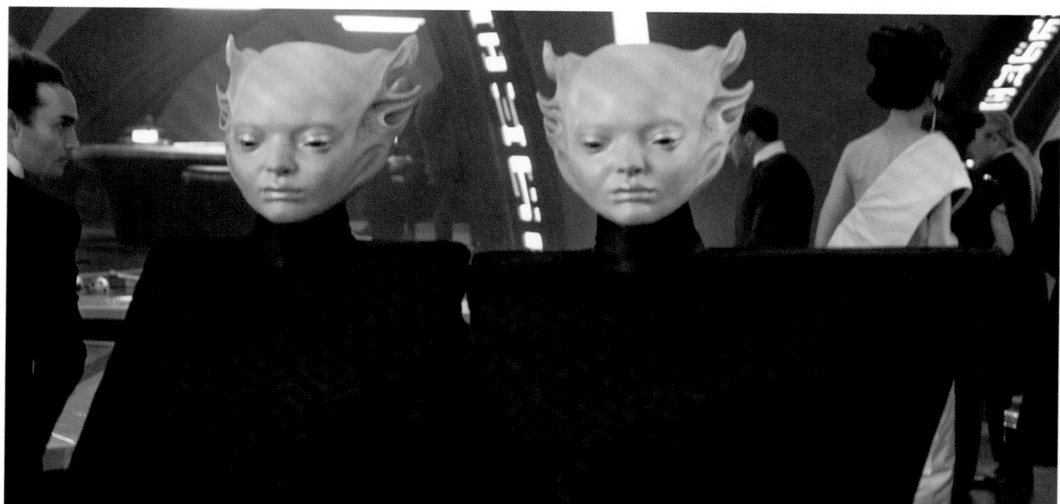

4 /

5 /

6 /

7 /

7 / Neepers Panpick

CREATING THE CASINO

Creating an environment that encompasses exotic fun with a barely concealed layer of greed and cruelty was a challenge met by the design team of *The Last Jedi.*

In a 1977 review of *Star Wars*, author J. G. Ballard wrote enthusiastically of its "ingenious and entertaining" visual ideas, and especially how the film depicts "an advanced technology in decline." It's an aesthetic that informs all three films in the original trilogy, but for the casino in Canto Bight in *The Last Jedi*, writer/director Rian Johnson was faced with a different challenge: how to depict luxury in the *Star Wars* universe.

For the location of Finn and Rose Tico's big adventure, Johnson's aim was to create "a Monte Carlo–like city that had to dazzle and seduce us." The task of developing the visuals of Canto Bight fell to production designer Rick Heinrichs, and "was by far the most involved design process in the movie" according to Johnson, who explains that "Heinrichs and his team worked to fuse visual cues from *Star Wars* into an entirely new feeling of wealth and opulence."

Heinrichs himself confirms that the aim was to create "an extremely extravagant, over-the-top version of Monte Carlo. We used a lot of architectural references to earlier *Star Wars* films, like columns and arches, but with more ovular, circular, softer shapes than what we've seen in the other films. I had read that Ralph McQuarrie, when he was working on Jabba's Palace, realized that if he kept with rectilinear forms it would look like a black castle from some 1930s swashbuckling movie, but if he kept to soft deco shapes, there's a real opportunity to come up with something fresh, an opulent quality, which would convey the idea of fun and beauty. That's what we were aiming for."

1 /

1 / A detailed look at the ornate casino set.

2 / Patrons enjoy a sophisticated evening's gambling at the casino accompnaied by an eloquent selection of popular tunes.

2 /

A HUGE GAMBLE

Not only was the Canto Bight Casino—which was constructed on the 007 Stage at Pinewood Studios in the U.K.—one of the biggest sets created for *The Last Jedi*, it was one of the most challenging. Supervising art director Chris Lowe makes note of how the team "had to create a very large cavernous gambling space with a bar in it for the action sequence. The scale of it was driven by the sequence itself and the scale of the fathiers, the creatures specific to the scene. We used lots of mirrors to throw the scale and keep the distance going."

Ultimately, the build, which took place over a 16-week period, was so large that it had to be split across two stages at Pinewood, with the exterior built at Longcross and the medieval city of Dubrovnik standing in for the city of Canto Bight, where the Casino is situated and where the action spills out. The sets were populated by hundreds of extras dressed to the nines by costume designer Michael Kaplan, along with numerous incredible creatures created and puppeteered by Neal Scanlan and his team, and rigged for action by SFX supervisor Chris Corbould and stunt coordinator Rob Inch. As Rian Johnson puts it, "It was a multi-department extravaganza!"

FINN
A MAN ON A MISSION

Everyone thinks he's a hero, but former stormtrooper Finn sure doesn't feel like one. The only thing he cares about is finding Rey and keeping her safe.

Abducted from his home planet, a young boy given the serial number FN-2187 was trained to become a First Order stormtrooper. Required to follow orders without question, he was sent into battle under the leadership of Captain Phasma, but he was unable to obey her directive.

When the opportunity arose to help captured Resistance pilot Poe Dameron escape from a First Order Star Destroyer, FN-2187 seized it. The pair hijacked a Special Forces TIE fighter and high-tailed it out of the ship. As they escaped, Dameron renamed his rescuer Finn. However, their daring getaway went awry when they were shot down and crash-landed back on Jakku.

Believing Poe was killed in the crash, Finn wandered the desert planet, eventually encountering Rey, a tough, young woman with a kind heart. Though Finn's only desire was to get as far away from the First Order as possible, when Rey was captured by the Order's Kylo Ren, Finn resolved to fight.

Aboard the *Millennium Falcon*, Finn journeyed to Starkiller Base, the First Order's superweapon. There, he tried to protect Rey from Ren, but was seriously injured during a lightsaber duel. Unconscious, Finn was brought aboard the *Falcon*, and he is later transferred to the Resistance flagship *Raddus*, where doctors place him in an emergency bacta suit to recover.

When Finn comes to, he is under the false impression that he is still on Starkiller Base. He is unaware that Rey has traveled to Ahch-To to train to become a Jedi, or that the Resistance fleet is being pursued across the galaxy by the First Order, which is on the verge of wiping them out. He's equally surprised to learn that everyone in the Resistance has heard his story: how he absconded from the First Order—the first time any stormtrooper has been known to do so—and helped destroy Starkiller Base. Not surprisingly, those in the Resistance believe he is a hero.

For his part, Finn isn't so sure. His only concern is in finding Rey and keeping her safe. As he attempts to leave the *Raddus*, he runs into maintenance worker Rose Tico. Together the pair devise a daring plan to help the Resistance fleet escape the First Order.

Once again, Finn is going to risk his life for the right cause—something that surely only a hero would do?

1 / Finn, back on his feet and ready for adventure! (See previous page)

2 / Showdown with Captain Phasma!

3 / Finn and BB-8 have struck up a friendship after a difficult start.

4 / Still recovering from wounds inflicted by Kylo Ren, Finn is awakened when the Resistance comes under attack. (See opposite page)

2 /

3 /

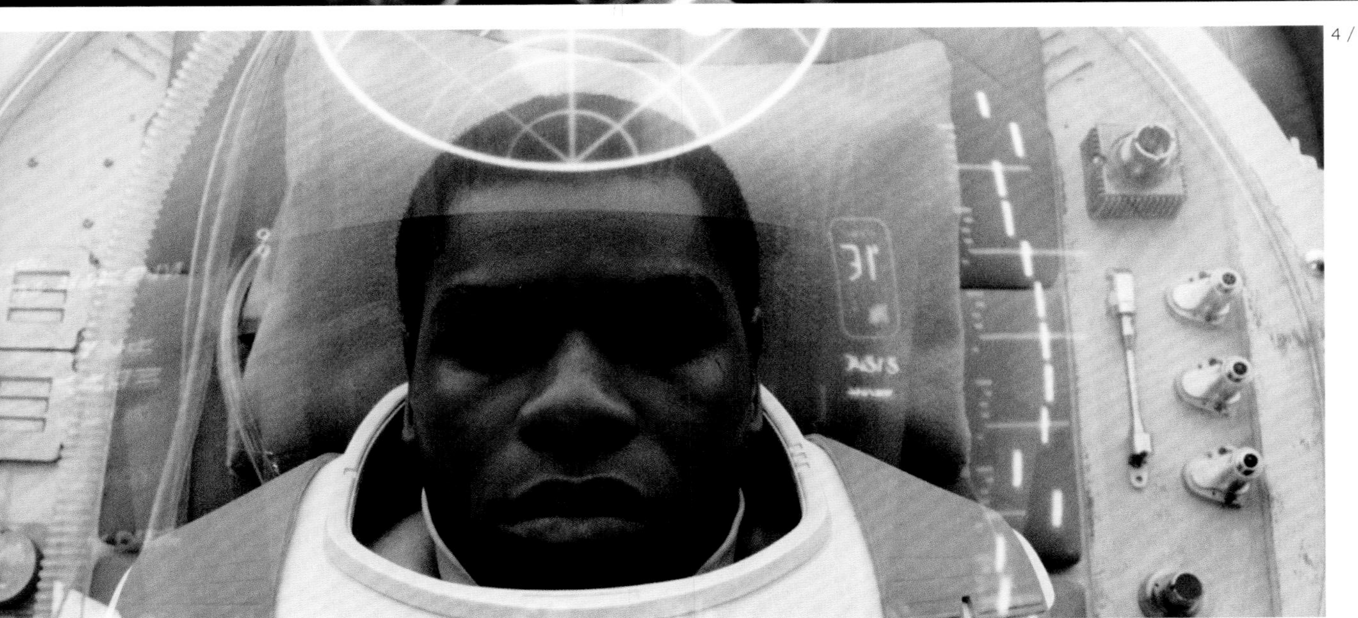

4 /

5 /

6 /

5 / Piloting a ski speeder as the Resistance makes a stand!

6 / Finn and the Resistance pilots race toward the First Order forces.

EVENING THE ODDS
JOHN BOYEGA

Healed after his near-fatal encounter with Kylo Ren, Finn is plunged into a mission, with the future of the Resistance at stake.

DIGGING DEEP

In getting to grips with the character of Finn in *The Last Jedi*, writer/director Rian Johnson looked back to the ex-stormtrooper's actions in *The Force Awakens*, where, though he fought alongside the Resistance, Finn was never actually a member. "Finn is motivated by personal emotion, not by ideological causes," says Johnson. "His bravery in *The Force Awakens* is to save his friend, not because he cares about her cause or Poe's army. In this film we're going to dig deeper in and see what he really believes in when the rubber meets the road."

Noting John Boyega's evident charisma, Johnson says that the actor "came to Finn in this movie with some real solidity and strength, and a bit of swagger in his step. He found an emerging strength in Finn that I loved watching develop."

1 /

1 / Finn takes a tumble as he discovers the city isn't all it seems.

2 / Finn faces his greatest challenge as he embarks on a daring mission for the Resistance. (See opposite page)

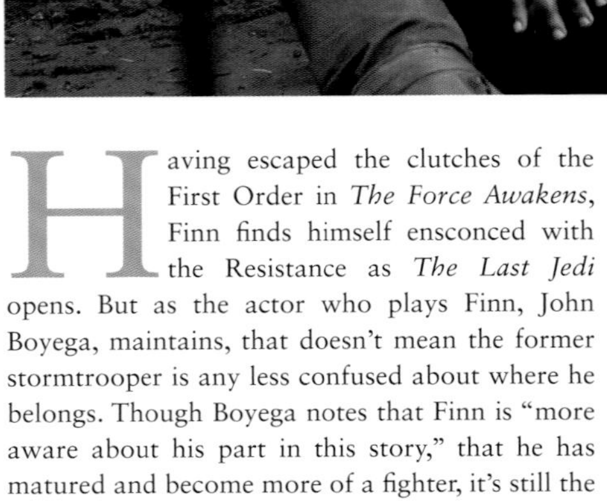

Having escaped the clutches of the First Order in *The Force Awakens*, Finn finds himself ensconced with the Resistance as *The Last Jedi* opens. But as the actor who plays Finn, John Boyega, maintains, that doesn't mean the former stormtrooper is any less confused about where he belongs. Though Boyega notes that Finn is "more aware about his part in this story," that he has matured and become more of a fighter, it's still the case that there are "some loose ends in terms of his character development."

One aspect of how Finn develops in *The Last Jedi* is his relationship with a new character, Resistance maintenance worker Rose Tico, played by Kelly Marie Tran. For Boyega it's a different kind of relationship to that between Finn and Rey, but it is anchored by a similar bond of "two people who are thrown together by circumstance and fate." As a consequence, Boyega states that "Finn and Rose make a really good team."

Another relationship that Boyega found rewarding on *The Last Jedi* was that between actor and director—i.e. between himself and Rian Johnson. Highlighting Johnson's fresh take on the *Star Wars* story, as well as his focus on each individual character and their personal tales, Boyega praises the director's "attention to detail" and "specific and honest" notes, along with his "sense of collaboration. I feel the best directors know how to collaborate, and he did just that."

As a confirmed *Star Wars* fan, and much as he did on *The Force Awakens*, Boyega had to work hard not to get distracted by the intricately detailed sets of *The Last Jedi*. "I was like a 12-year-old kid at Disneyland, but Disneyland was on level 10," he says. "That's just what it was like, but then you had to do your job because you were part of the story. I tried to take it all in as a fan whilst remaining professional about my role in the film. Ultimately, I think I did well with the balance, but it was crazy because there was so much going on. There were both major sets and practical effects to navigate. The crew outdid themselves with the sets they built. It made me feel like I was on another planet, which was very good."

3 / Finn takes on Phasma
as FN-2187 confronts
his former captain.

ROSE TICO
WORKING FOR THE GOOD GUYS

Like her sister Paige, Rose Tico has harbored a simmering hatred for the First Order ever since she was a child. Now she finally has the chance to fight back.

Raised by their parents Hue and Thanya in the Otomok system, Rose Tico and her older sister Paige grew up in the peaceful mining colony of Hays Minor. The girls dreamed of leaving their home and traveling the galaxy, of experiencing its myriad marvels...until the First Order arrived and crushed those dreams.

Unbeknownst to the Galactic Republic, the nefarious military organization began razing the cities of Otomok to test their armaments. They abducted the planet's children for recruitment purposes and left the survivors nothing to live for—except perhaps their burning hatred of the First Order.

Wearing twin medallions adorned with the symbol of the Otomok system, Paige and Rose joined the Resistance cause—the former serving as a ventral gunner aboard a bomber, the latter as a member of the support crew. A talented mechanic, Rose developed a system that makes the Resistance's spacecraft harder for enemy sensors to detect. After the evacuation of D'Qar, she guards the *Raddus*' escape pods from anyone who tries to flee.

Even before they meet him, the Tico sisters know of Finn's story. To them, his actions proved that he is a real hero—one who knew right from wrong, and who didn't simply run away when he had the chance.

When they realize the First Order has the ability to track the Resistance fleet through hyperspace, Finn and Rose devise a plan to sneak aboard the enemy's flagship and disable the tracker. In order to accomplish this, they need a codebreaker. The only place they can locate one is the casino city of Canto Bight on Cantonica: a dangerous planet populated by war profiteers and criminals...

2 /

3 /

4 /

1 / Rose Tico of the Resistance. (See previous page)

2 / Rose and Finn team up on a mission for the Resistance.

3 / Finn meets an initially less-than-friendly Rose!

4 / Rose confronts Finn in the casino city Canto Bight.

5 / Rose embarks on a life or death mission. (See opposite page)

TECH SAVVY
KELLY MARIE TRAN

A brave and resourceful young woman, Rose Tico rides with Finn into action and serves as his moral guide.

ROSE BY ANY OTHER NAME

To Rian Johnson's way of thinking, each character in the *Star Wars* saga "reflects some part of how we all feel, or at least how we'd like to feel." Rose Tico, however, "is the closest to how 10-year-old me would have felt if he woke up in this universe. She doesn't belong here, but she's going to be brave and do her best. Luckily we found the perfect embodiment of that spirit with Kelly Marie Tran. I love her to death, and I'm thrilled to introduce audiences to both Rose and Kelly."

4 /

A new introduction to the *Star Wars* universe, Rose Tico is part of the support crew working on the Resistance starfighters. Rose is played in *The Last Jedi* by Kelly Marie Tran, who highlights the fact that Rose has an older sister, Paige, who is a gunner for the Resistance—a more traditionally heroic role. Rose, says Tran, "is the opposite of that. She works in maintenance, and she's a nobody. Her sister's always been the cool one that's been out there in the forefront of the action. Rose has always been the one behind pipes, fixing things."

Until, that is, events early on in *The Last Jedi*, at which point Rose's life changes drastically. As part of that, she meets Finn, who Tran describes as "a big deal to her," likening him to "a childhood hero. Rose has always been someone who has been on the bottom of the food chain in the Resistance. And here is Finn, someone who, for her, represents why she's there. So they meet and go on a series of crazy adventures together."

Expressing her excitement at becoming a *Star Wars* heroine and getting to stand alongside a group of similarly strong females, not just in *The Last Jedi* but across the whole saga, Tran nevertheless admits to feeling some trepidation. While she hopes Rose will be a role model, she also feels the weight of responsibility: "You just wanted to do it right. And you wanted to do the franchise right, because so many generations love this thing."

The actress recalls experiencing a similar level of excitement when she first landed the role of Rose Tico in *The Last Jedi*, as well as the torture of having to keep the exciting news a secret. "I found out that I got the role in November of 2015," she says. "I moved to London in December immediately after that, but I couldn't tell anybody where I was going or what I was actually doing until February 2016. I lied to everybody I knew and said I was in Canada working on an indie movie."

4 / Rose and Finn witness decadance on a galactic scale at the casino on Canto Bight.

5 / Resistance heroine Rose Tico on a dangerous mission. (See opposite page)

DJ

SHOW HIM THE MONEY

Con artists can be found in any prison in the galaxy, and they all have something in common: It's best not to trust them!

The assorted thieves and pickpockets who wind up in the Canto Bight jail ordinarily don't plan on getting caught…all except for one. Unlikely as it seems, DJ actually lets the local police arrest him on purpose; for as he explains to all his cellmates, jail is the only place where he can sleep without worrying about the authorities.

A cynical survivor and a self-proclaimed victim of societal inequity, DJ only cares about one thing: money. Such is his mercenary nature that he would happily work for the Resistance or the First Order, his choice determined by how much money he would make out of the deal.

That kind of attitude perfectly reflects his only belief, as well as his nickname: Don't Join. To DJ, following a greater cause like the Resistance or the First Order is a game. Sooner or later, followers of either end up dead—and DJ will do anything he can to survive.

While he's been accused of many things, being a bad codebreaker is not one of them. With his modified Zinbiddle card, DJ can crack open the cell doors of the Canto Bight jail at any time he feels, while his specially handcrafted keys can temporarily bypass even bio-hexacrypt-protected data networks.

TRUST ISSUES
BENICIO DEL TORO

The strange underworld profiteer DJ doesn't trust anyone, but can Finn and Rose trust *him*?

THIS CHARMING MAN

Director Rian Johnson admits to feeling fortunate that Benicio Del Toro agreed to play the part of DJ in *The Last Jedi*, adding: "He's charming but also rides that wonderful line where you're not exactly sure if you trust him." According to costume designer Michael Kaplan, Del Toro's outfit in the film helped the actor discover who and what DJ is. "His costume had a big collar that he started hiding behind," says Kaplan. "Cool boots and gloves, all these things he found a way to use in creating his character."

1 /

1 / Always in trouble, never to blame!

2 / DJ as played by Benicio Del Toro. (See opposite page)

Joining a long lineage of scoundrels stretching back to the original *Star Wars*, Benicio Del Toro plays DJ, a dubious and enigmatic figure encountered by Finn and Rose in a jail cell on Canto Bight.

Del Toro describes DJ as "very cool," but also "a cynic," explaining: "He believes that good guys and bad guys are just basically the same." In addition, the actor makes note of the fact that DJ is "a profiteer. He profits from the eternal war of good and evil. He's an opportunist but can get you out of a jam, and get you in a jam. We play that line of whether he is good or bad. We don't know. But he's a mercenary, really."

For Del Toro, the opportunity to get to grips with a shady *Star Wars* character who both plays to and against audience expectations was one that he relished. Calling the production "a winning team," the actor highlights how "they allowed creativity to grow in front of the camera. Creating a character like this is really fun."

Developing DJ entailed working closely with writer/director Rian Johnson. According to Del Toro, Johnson is the kind of director you can get creative with. "I had ideas and ran them by Rian," the actor explains. "And Rian is a fun director that way." The aim for the pair was "to build something that was unique for this film. At the same time, DJ had to be both repulsive and attractive. So you juggle that and hope some things work better than others. But I had faith in Rian."

As Del Toro's explains, "DJ's mantra is live free and don't join." It's an attitude that DJ attempts to use to persuade Finn to his way of thinking, "to show Finn that even the good guys are dirty at times and perhaps corrupt as well. He's like this little devil on Finn's shoulder that basically is trying to make him see a different side or different approach to living in the galaxy."

DRESSED FOR SUCCESS

To fit in with the high society, you have to look the part. Michael Kaplan was tailor to the rich and the beautiful of Canto Bight.

1/

2 /

3 /

WEIRD AND WONDERFUL

Working in concert with costume designer Michael Kaplan, hair and makeup designer Peter Swords King endeavored to ensure the casino patrons' costumes and hair complemented one another. King designed somewhere between 400 and 500 hairstyles, but only 60 were used. "A lot we pushed out because they just weren't *Star Wars*-looking enough," he says. "They didn't look intergalactic. They looked too ordinary. We wanted extraordinary, almost impractical, impossible hairstyles and makeup. It took us about six months to get all these styles and looks whittled down."

Another aspect of the casino customers' look were the subtle prosthetics King and his team designed. These additions and alterations—including the removal of many extras' eyebrows—are barely noticeable, but were important in making the characters look "odd," according to King. "A good third of the women had all their eyebrows blocked out. We didn't put new ones in. And it just makes them look strange. If you take someone's eyebrows away, it's the oddest thing."

He adds, "It was designing with concept designers, scrolling through books, taking influence from the 1960s and '70s and adapting those. But then, just some really crazy, wacky ideas. It was brilliant fun."

4 /

5 /

A vital aspect of making the casino scenes a success were the costumes worn by the extras. Costume designer Michael Kaplan and his team made hundreds of costumes, each one completely different, requiring a huge and time-consuming effort to source fabrics from New York to Los Angeles, and from London to Florence. Keeping in mind the black-and-white theme Rian Johson had alighted on, Kaplan set about finding prints that would fit into the *Star Wars* vernacular. The team even utilized a milliner, which Kaplan believes is a first for *Star Wars*, along with specialized makers of jewelry and gloves.

Kaplan made a point of choosing the extras for the casino himself, picking the kinds of interesting, exotic faces that might fit the *Star Wars* universe. The costume designer reports he was looking for "sophistication, good posture, and exoticism. We were able to design costumes specifically for the individuals we'd chosen."

1 / Baron Yasto Attsmun and Ubialla Gheal aboard the *Undisputed Victor*. (See opposite page)

2 / Glamor is the order of the day as Dynym Quid (right) arrives.

3 / Vylla Tendeil beguiles.

4 / Grayla Stindy (in white) with an unamed Abednedo companion.

5 / Centada Ressad dons an alluring headpiece.

CASINO CREATURES

Neal Scanlan and his team were tasked with creating the space oddities drawn to Canto Bight by the allure of fun and profit.

CREATURE CREATORS

Of all the various departments director Rian Johnson needed to keep an eye on during the making of *The Last Jedi*, his favorite to review was creature designer Neal Scanlan's workshop. Scanlan had a huge task, as the number of creatures he and his team had to design for the film was vast. Johnson likens the workshop to Willy Wonka's Chocolate Factory, recalling how the design process would begin with sketches, which would be turned into sculptures, and finally working puppets. "You could get six inches away and look into its eyes, and it looked like a real, living creature. It was just absolutely extraordinary."

Calling Scanlan and his team "superstars," Johnson states: "Their reverence for the art of creature creation is present in every single one of their works, and it was an honor getting to collaborate with them."

1 /

As the designer of the special creature effects for *The Last Jedi* and the man in charge of all the practical creatures, Neal Scanlan had his work cut out when it came to the scenes at the casino in Canto Bight. Not only were there a huge number of new creatures to create, but these patrons of the casino had to reflect the glitz and glamor of their surroundings.

"We're used to seeing the skullduggery and the grungier side of *Star Wars*," says Scanlan, "but less used to seeing the high rollers of the galaxy. It was quite a trick to hold on to the *Star Wars* DNA while taking it to a place we hadn't been to before."

The creatures Scanlan and his team created for the casino ranged from ones with animatronic heads, to mechanical puppets, to hand puppets, to remote controlled puppets dangling from the ceiling, and the results were remarkable. Scanlan himself recalls the experience of stepping into the casino as "breathtaking" and "a delight," adding: "It is the final confirmation at every level. That's the first time we got to step back and see not only our department, but all the other departments' aspirations and vision for the film come together. There can't be many people who didn't walk on that set and take a breath. From the set to the props, everything about it was incredible. And you played a part in that."

1 / Kedpin Shoklop prepares for a massage at the famous Zord's spa. (See opposite page)

2 / Kaljach Sonmi plays it cool.

3 / Ganzer tends the bar.

4 / Letrun Pay soaks up the atmosphere.

5 / Count Sosear Latta, a regular at the casino.

6 / Wealthy beach-dweller Slowen Lo.

7 / The hard face of casino security, Pemmin Brunce makes sure that nobody is cheating.

FORMING THE FATHIERS

Large and fast, the fathiers were created using an ingenious mixture of practical effects and computer-generated imagery.

AN EMOTIONAL MOMENT

Recalling the moment he first witnessed a full-size, finished fathier being brought to life by puppeteers on set, writer/director Rian Johnson exclaims: "I've never experienced anything like it. They took this robot covered with latex and rubber and yak hair, and when they worked their magic you could stand three feet away from it, nose to nose, and you'd swear it was a living, breathing thing. It conveyed real emotion."

1 /

1 / A fathier 'performs' an emotional scene.

2 / The stables on Canto Bight provide shelter to the creatures. (See opposite page)

Of all the creatures created for *The Last Jedi*, the most striking are the fathiers. These horse-like, feline-featured animals (with a hint of lion and owl) stand almost 16 feet tall, and as such represented quite the challenge, not just in terms of the animatronics required for their distinctive movements, but the mechanization needed for their wonderfully expressive faces.

The creation of the fathiers required close collaboration between creature designer Neal Scanlan and his team and the team at ILM. Aaron McBride from ILM provided early concepts, from which Scanlan and team built a full-sized maquette, covered with flocked body fur and hand-punched mane, tail, belly and ankle hair. Once approved, this design formed the basis of a head and shoulder puppet featured in the stable reveal shots and formed the initial design for ILM's CG fathier build.

Each final CG fathier was covered with more than 10 million hand-groomed hairs, dynamic mane and tail and all covered with layers of CG dirt particles. Internally, the fathiers contained a CG skeleton, muscles, surrounding fat layer and sliding skin over the top, designed to convey the incredible agility and weight of the creatures.

When it came to putting the fathier sequence together, one of the most challenging aspects was working out how to place actors on the back of a CG fathier and then composite both elements back into real film plates, along with the rest of the rampaging CG fathier herd. This complexity demanded that all three departments—visual effects, creature effects and special effects—work very closely together. ILM built a full-size, articulated body section with saddle, and mounted it on a 6-axis motion base. This whole system was then programmed directly from ILM's animation scenes, including a Bolt robot camera system that afforded very dynamic camera movements within the interactive lighting dome they built around the riding rig and actors. Taking such care to drive the practical fathier rig with approved CG animation meant that every practical bump, jump, lurch and skid felt by the actors directly matched the final animation of the CG character in the shot.

THE FIRST ORDER

Intent on seizing military control of the galaxy, the First Order is a deadly threat to the Resistance. Here, we take a look at its various ranks...

SUPREME LEADER SNOKE

Snoke's name is feared throughout the galaxy, and although his reputation precedes him, there are very few who have seen him in person. He uses obscurity and deception to instill fear, such as his immense visual projections, which hide his physical frailties and misshapen face. Although Snoke is not a Sith Lord, he is powerful in the dark side of the Force, with the ability to persuade, manipulate and perceive people in the far reaches of space.

SNOKE
THE SUPREME LEADER

A shadowy figure at the heart of the First Order, little is known about the mysterious, wizened leader who is poised to crush the Resistance and take control of the galaxy.

Force sensitive, and highly attuned to the dark side but not a Sith, Snoke has trained Kylo Ren and at least one other apprentice.

Snoke believed General Leia Organa and Han Solo's son Ben (the grandson of Darth Vader and nephew of Jedi Master Luke Skywalker) to be adept with the dark side. He exerted his terrible influence on the young boy, corrupting him.

While his mother was aware of the influence Snoke had on Ben, she kept this from Han, believing he would not understand. Leia felt it was her role to keep Ben away from the dark side.

Eventually, Snoke turned Ben away from the light side, renaming him Kylo Ren, master of the Knights of Ren. As Ren, he carried out his master's will in destroying Luke's newly revived Jedi Order. Ren killed many of his fellow students, but Skywalker managed to escape and went into hiding. Snoke assigned Ren the job of hunting him down.

As Ren's search intensified, General Armitage Hux suggested to Snoke that he use the First Order's superweapon, Starkiller Base, to destroy the New Republic government. Agreeing to this, Snoke then ordered Ren to kill his father to overcome his temptation by the light side.

Shortly after the destruction of the Hosnian system, the center of the New Republic, Ren captured Rey—a scavenger who had seen the final piece of the map which revealed Skywalker's location—intending to use the Force to make her reveal the location to him. Snoke was disturbed to hear that the woman resisted Ren's interrogation. Ren explained she was strong in the Force, but evidently untrained.

Snoke ordered Hux to destroy the Resistance before Skywalker could be found, and instructed Ren to bring Rey to him. But Rey managed to escape with the help of her new, burgeoning powers. As Starkiller Base was destroyed, Snoke demanded Hux escort Ren to him in order to complete his training.

Aboard the Mega-class Star Destroyer, the *Supremacy*, Snoke commands his vast army. In a show of strength and power, he addresses members of the First Order by broadcasting a towering image of himself from his throne room. Rarely appearing in public, he is protected by eight Praetorian Guards: loyal, fearsome warriors clad in red robes and armor who stand ready to defend him against attack.

PRAETORIAN GUARD

THE LAST LINE OF DEFENSE

Dressed in distinctive red combat armor reminiscent of the Emperor's loyal soldiers, the Praetorian Guards stand at the ready in Snoke's throne room..

Their origins shrouded in mystery, Snoke's elite warriors seemingly possess no individual identities. Standing motionless in the throne room, they only take action when the Supreme Leader is endangered. These implacable, loyal, ever-vigilant sentinels protect Snoke from whoever may represent a threat, be it his guests, generals, or even his apprentice, Kylo Ren.

When activated, the Praetorians' layered red armor produces an intense local magnetic field that deflects blaster fire and even glancing lightsaber blows. Their tempered metal blades are made even more lethal by a high-frequency vibration created across the cutting edge by a compact ultrasonic generator. In addition, the energized blade parallel to each cutting edge can parry a lightsaber.

EIGHT COMBATANTS

There are four pairs of sentinels in the Praetorian Guard, and each pair wields the same weapons —high-tech versions of ancient analog weapons from across the galaxy: an electro-bisento, a vibro-voulge, a bilari electro-chain whip, and twin vibro-arbir blades.

THE PRAETORIAN GUARD

Crimson warriors who protect Supreme Leader Snoke, the Praetorian Guard rely on an assortment of high-tech archaic weapons, along with a hybrid fighting style of unarmed combat techniques. Made up of four pairs, they are the last line of defense against Snoke's enemies.

IN COMBAT

The Praetorian Guard carry deadly weapons that have an ultrasonic generator to increase the cutting edge's lethality, and energised blades capable of parrying lightsabers. Their laminate armor is constructed with heavy plates, and impregnated with conductive wirepaths that can deflect blaster fire with its magnetised energy field which, although painful to the wearer, they endure with painstaking loyalty and devotion.

KYLO REN
COMMITTED TO THE DARK SIDE

He has sacrificed everything to become the dark lord his master wishes him to be, and yet there is still conflict within Kylo Ren.

The Force is strong with Ben Solo. The son of Leia—daughter of Darth Vader and sister of Luke Skywalker—Ben trained to become a Jedi under the guidance of his uncle Luke. But the darkness swiftly rose in him, and Ben was soon seduced to the dark side by the shadowy Snoke, taking the name Kylo Ren. The malign influence of the First Order's Supreme Leader sent the young man down an ever darker path, leading him to destroy the Jedi training temple, to reject his family, and finally to murder his own father, Han Solo, on Starkiller Base.

Shortly after committing patricide, and before the mobile ice planet was destroyed, Ren faced Rey in the woods which surrounded the base. As they fought, Rey bested him, severely wounding him in single combat.

Rescued by General Hux, Kylo Ren returned to his master, to find Snoke manifestly disappointed. Snoke taunted his apprentice, further destabilizing the young man's already fractured mind. As an obedient servant, Ren follows Snoke's orders to pursue and crush the fleeing Resistance, but the words of his father echo in his mind—that Snoke is merely using him for his power.

Fueled by the dark side, Ren's ambition drives him to desire more, to plan on taking the place he thinks he deserves in the First Order. But there's something else he cannot ignore. He and the scavenger from Jakku share a strange bond in the Force, a mysterious connection whose true nature and meaning Kylo Ren is still attempting to comprehend...

2 /

1 / The ever-conflicted Kylo Ren. (See previous page)

2 / The sinister helmet masks the rage beneath.

3 / Ren surveys the military might of the First Order.

4 / Leading the attack aboard his TIE silencer.

3 /

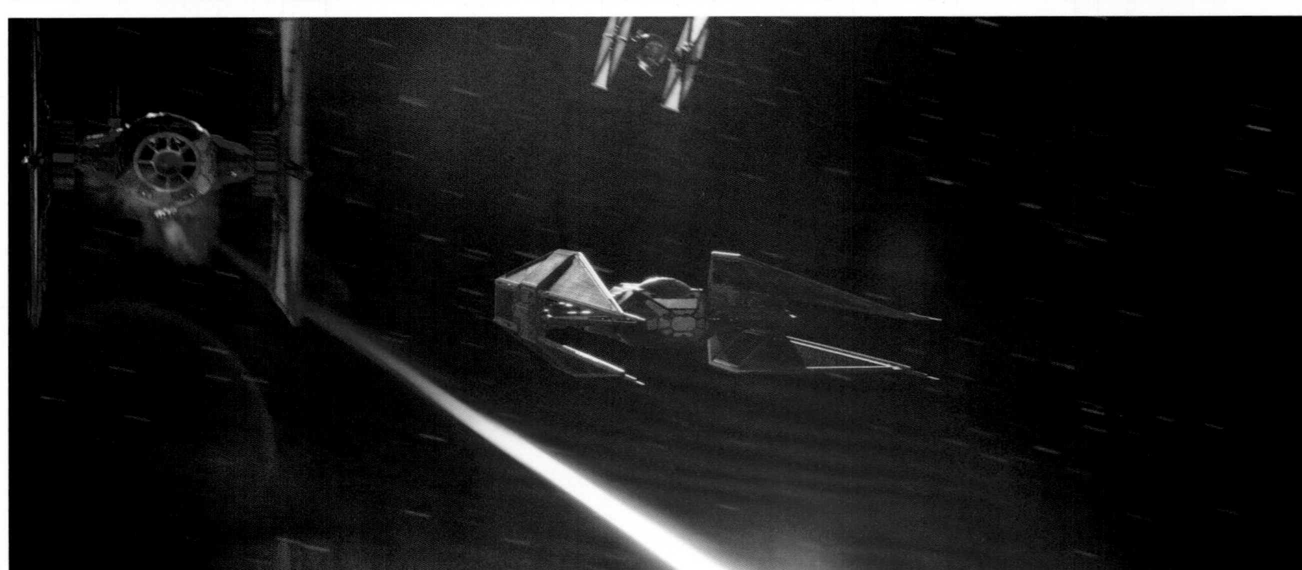

4 /

KYLO REN

The Supreme Leader's apprentice faces constant berating from his master for his failings. Scarred physically and emotionally, Kylo's tactical reasoning is often clouded by rage and resentment, fuelling his rise to power. Kylo Ren chooses to form his own dark destiny, built on his feelings of isolation and mistrust for those close to him. He is a skilled pilot, like his father and grandfather, mercilessly deployed in his TIE silencer.

5 / Kylo Ren at his most dangerous.

GENERAL HUX

THE MILITARY MASTERMIND

The brutal commander whose machinations have caused billions of deaths will not let the destruction of Starkiller Base be the end of his thirst for power.

Armitage Hux craves power above all else. The son of Imperial general Brendol Hux, Armitage didn't hesitate to eliminate his father when it became evident he represented a threat to his ascent to command.

Raised to the rank of general, Hux became the key man in Snoke's military strategy—and one of the few individuals with direct access to him. Placed in charge of Starkiller Base, the young general suggested to the Supreme Leader that they test the superweapon embedded in the ice planet and destroy the only obstacle standing in their way: the New Republic.

As he informed his troops during a passionate speech, after the disappearance of the senate, all systems would bow to the First Order. And he was correct: Even with the destruction of Starkiller Base by the Resistance, no underground movement, no planet, no system could possibly match the might of the First Order.

Moreover, Hux's engineers have developed another insidious technological breakthrough: active hyperspace tracking. With the ability to locate Resistance ships as they travel through hyperspace, Hux knows it's only a matter of time before he and the First Order can put an end to their last opponent and finally rule the galaxy.

But the obliteration of the Resistance is not Hux's only concern. Fuelled by an unquenchable thirst for power, the general surreptitiously plans his next move from the bridge of his flagship, the *Resurgent*-class Star Destroyer the *Finalizer*. And all the while he is careful to keep his thoughts hidden from both Snoke and Kylo Ren, lest his ideas of betrayal be discovered.

CAPTAIN PHASMA

ARMORED SYMBOL OF POWER

Taken as children from conquered worlds and trained to serve the First Order, stormtroopers fight to restore order and stability—and Captain Phasma is their most feared commander.

Hailing from the harsh, primitive world of Parnassos, Phasma grew up a member of a merciless tribe whose followers were forced to kill in order to survive. When the First Order subjugated her planet, she joined its ranks to escape her savage and cruel existence.

Swearing loyalty to the First Order and its cause, Phasma developed into an unforgiving commander. She led the assault on Jakku in an attempt to retrieve the map to Luke Skywalker's location before the Resistance acquired it. When stormtrooper FN-2187 failed to carry out her orders, little did she suspect that he would go even further and desert, in the process freeing Resistance pilot Poe Dameron from prison.

Phasma and the rebellious stormtrooper crossed paths on Starkiller Base, where Finn—the traitor's new name—threatened to shoot her if she refused to take down the base shields, thus opening the way for Poe and his squadron of starfighters. Surviving the destruction of Starkiller Base, Phasma eliminated all traces of her treason, even going so far as to murder Lieutenant Sol Rivas, who could have reported her. Now Phasma waits, ready for the next opportunity to confront the anomaly FN-2187.

To accomplish that, Phasma will need to make full use of her chromium-plated armor, forged from the hull of a Naboo vessel once owned by the Emperor (and later used by General Hux's father); her combat quicksilver baton, made of a collapsible micromesh matrix, which can expand or condense at will; and her blaster rifle and customized SE-44C blaster pistol.

CAPTAIN PHASMA

Captain Phasma stands as a symbol of the First Order's regime, in her unique chromium-plated armor. Hailing from a primitive planet of harsh terrain and a kill-or-be-killed lifestyle, Phasma's only goal is survival, having killed fellow ranking officers and conspiring against political rivals in the First Order. She is completely combat ready, with a custom targeting system in her helmet, emergency cyrothoric acid, a collapsible quicksilver baton and powerful blasters.

STORMTROOPERS

SOLDIERS OF THE FIRST ORDER

From stormtroopers to Praetorian guards, the First Order's army is on the rise.

STORMTROOPER

The distinctive armor of the stormtroopers has evolved over the years but has always inspired fear across the galaxy.

The men and women who serve in the First Order have been trained all of their lives to bring stability by means of strength to the galaxy in accordance with Supreme Leader Snoke's will.

EXECUTIONER TROOPER

Any standard stormtrooper can be assigned the role of executioner, because all stormtroopers have been trained to administer capital punishment without hesitation. Their laser ax brings instant justice via its razor-sharp energy ribbons, extended from a quartet of collapsible claws.

TIE FIGHTER PILOT

Eager to prove their worth after the destruction of Starkiller Base, which was thought to be down to the poor TIE fighter defense, TIE pilots are particularly driven to track down and destroy the Resistance. They will hold nothing back in a bid to make them suffer.

FLAMETROOPER

Brandishing D-93 Incinerators, the flametroopers are trained to rain fire on enemies of the First Order. They are equipped with flame-proof armor.

SNOWTROOPER

Trained for combat in freezing conditions, the snowtroopers are deployed to Crait. Although not a cold world, the planet features conditions that require specific training and specialized equipment.

Stormtroopers of the First Order: a terrifying symbol of power and cruelty in the galaxy.

FIRST STRIKE

The First Order may have lost its most devastating weapon, but they still have a powerful arsenal ready to strike back against the Resistance.

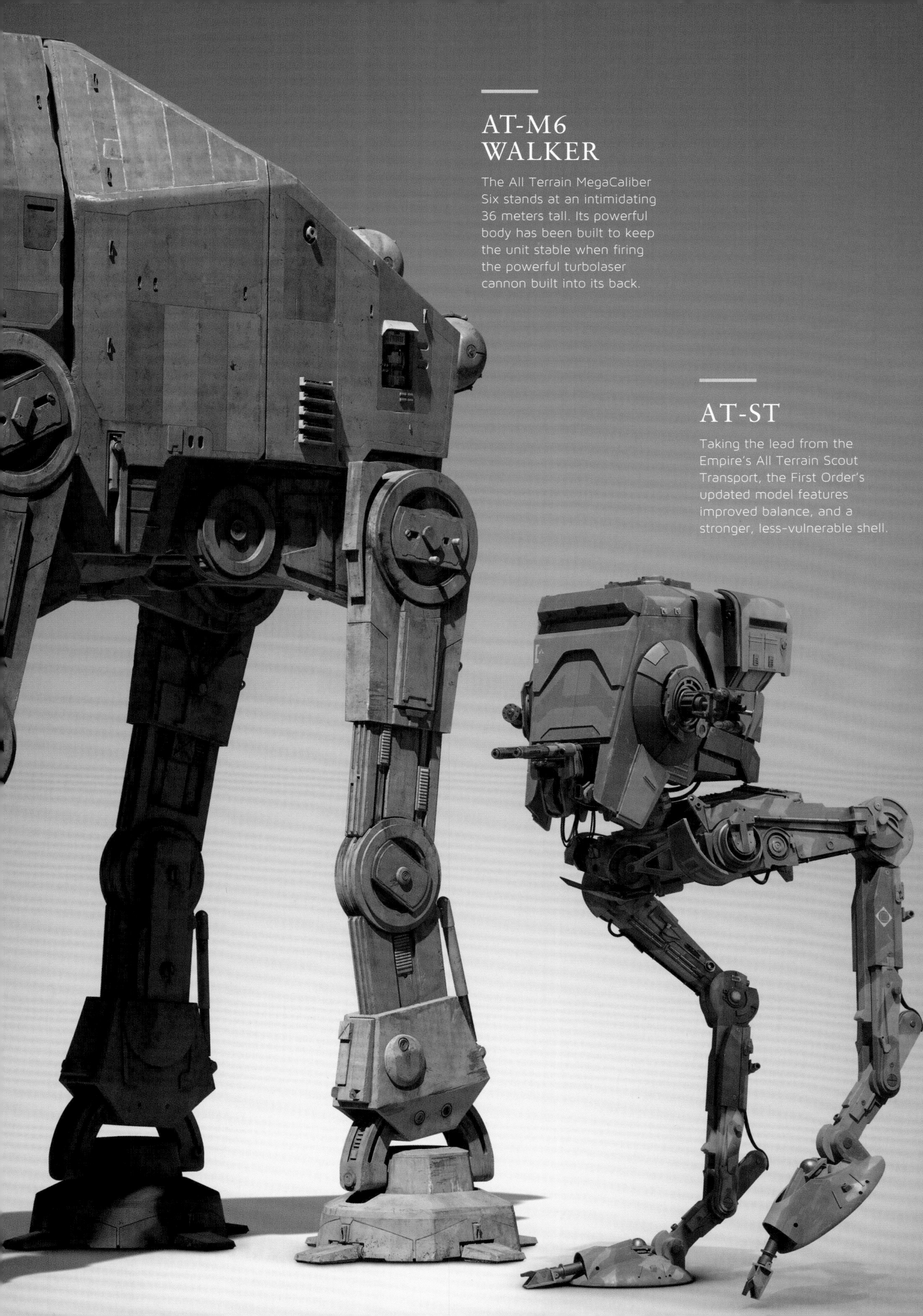

AT-M6 WALKER

The All Terrain MegaCaliber Six stands at an intimidating 36 meters tall. Its powerful body has been built to keep the unit stable when firing the powerful turbolaser cannon built into its back.

AT-ST

Taking the lead from the Empire's All Terrain Scout Transport, the First Order's updated model features improved balance, and a stronger, less-vulnerable shell.

THE *FINALIZER*

The enormous command ship of General Hux is at the forefront of the siege of D'Qar.

TIE SILENCER

A prototype ship, this formidable craft is piloted by Kylo Ren as he leads Special Forces in their attack on the *Raddus*.

TIE/SF FIGHTER

Despite being fast and maneuverable, the TIE fighter defence of the Starkiller Base was found wanting, leaving the surviving pilots with a lot to prove.

UPSILON COMMAND SHUTTLE

An imposing craft, used by high-ranking First Order officers, including Kylo Ren.

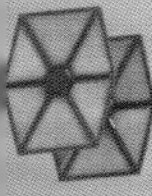

SHOWDOWN ON CRAIT

Cornered by the First Order, the Resistance is forced to improvise as the enemy prepares to strike the final blow. Take a look behind the scenes at this incredible sequence...

2 /

An important new environment that we visit in the movie is the mineral world Crait. Rian Johnson had a very specific visual idea for its look from the inception of the story. "It would have a thin, white layer of salt that's like a topsoil," the director explains. "But under that would be a ruby-red crystal foundation. It offered incredible possibilities for an alien environment that we hadn't seen before."

Production designer Rick Heinrichs worked with Rian Johnson to give Crait a magmatic layer of red mineral coated by salt flakes on its white surface. When the surface is disturbed, the red shows to give a distinctive great red and white design graphic. The landscape was created on a stage at Pinewood Studios and later matched in with a plate-shoot on the salt flats of Bolivia.

The crystal foxes, known as vulptices, living on Crait serve a very specific story function in the movie. Their design speaks to the type of creature that one might expect to see on a mineral planet where it rains salt. They evolved with crystalline fur, almost like when you put a stick in sugar water and it forms candy crystals. The vulptices are ultimately executed as hand-animated CG characters and feature shimmering 'fur' coats of clear crystal shards brought to life by the visual effects team.

Creature designer Neal Scanlan went to some extraordinary lengths to get an initial idea of what the vulptices may look and be shaped like. "We had a taxidermy form of a fox and created a clay sculpture that we added straw to, in order to see how you'd replace hair," says Scanlan. "Then, we tried to find a balance between something that was solid and heavy but also soft and appealing. I saw the vulptices as a predominantly female species. There were some

1 / AT-M6 walkers march across Crait, disturbing the surface layer. (See previous page)

2 / Poe Dameron leads the charge to engage the enemy.

3 / Rey uses the Force to help the Resistance survivors escape. (See opposite page)

3 /

4 /

4 / Snowtroopers storm the base.

5 / A defensive trench reveals the red mineral beneath the surface. (See opposite page)

6 / Soldiers man the trenches. (See opposite page)

7 / The battle takes its toll on the tired army. (See opposite page)

8 / A tiny spark of hope regained for the Resistance? (See opposite page)

beautiful images we found of female foxes. The team assigned to the project worked through three or four iterations of what they might look like. Rian kept pushing us toward making them sparkle, with a more crystal-like appearance."

The design by ILM's Art Department features crystal foxes with prominent horns and signature crystal whiskers. Their bodies are covered in a sparkling iridescent coat of clear crystal fur. Hero crystals on the face, back and tail were positioned by hand in the computer. The rest of the body was covered by procedurally growing thousands of curves over the surface of the creature and then replacing them with "crystal shards and quills" of different shapes and sizes at render time. Finally, ILM's groom artist applied shorter, softer hairs to fill in any gaps. All in all, there were about 25,000 CG crystals on each fox.

Next came giving the foxes movement. Referencing real animals such as Arctic foxes, ILM's animation team keyframe-animated the CG foxes, rigged with an internal muscle system and face-shape controls. Individual crystal movement relative to their size/weight and surrounding environment ensured no collisions occurred as the skittish creatures moved around their alien world.

Summing up his experience on *The Last Jedi,* Neal Scanlan says, "I can only describe it as being given an opportunity a second time around. It was as if the first time around was practice. First you practice, and then you put that practice into practical and see where you can go.

5 /

6 /

7 /

8 /

I really do hope the directors continue to be demanding and understanding [in future films]. Having a strong creative pulse will benefit future films and will really give *Star Wars* fans something to look forward to, which will be absolutely amazing.

Visual Effects supervisor Ben Morris reflects on what he and his team accomplish through their art, not just on *The Last Jedi* but on modern films in general: "Increasingly in film-making, visual effects is not just a tool to create magic. It's becoming a Swiss army knife tool kit. We can modify things in shots and even change the weather, so we're indirectly helping all departments in the film, which is why nowadays VFX crews are enormous. We're not just creating aliens, spaceships and dinosaurs anymore."

9 /

10 /

11 /

12 /

9 / A vulptex surveys the plains of Crait. (See opposite page)

10 / Kylo Ren orders the death of Luke Skywalker. (See opposite page)

11 / Facing off against Luke in a tense confrontation.

12 / A ski speeder roars into action.

SCORING *STAR WARS*

One of the *Star Wars* saga's most crucial features is the score, written, as ever, by John Williams.

In a career spanning 60 years (and counting), legendary composer John Williams has scored some of the biggest films ever made—and for more than 40 of those years, those films have included eight episodes of the ongoing *Star Wars* saga.

One of America's most accomplished and successful composers for film and the concert stage, Williams has served as music director and laureate conductor of one of the country's treasured musical institutions, the Boston Pops Orchestra, and maintains thriving artistic relationships with many of the world's great orchestras, including the Boston Symphony Orchestra, the New York Philharmonic, the Chicago Symphony Orchestra and the Los Angeles Philharmonic. Among the prestigious awards he has received are the National Medal of Arts; the Kennedy Center Honors; the Olympic Order; and numerous Academy Awards, GRAMMY Awards, Emmy Awards and Golden Globe Awards.

Williams' music has become synonymous with *Star Wars*, and his score for *The Last Jedi* is as sweeping and characteristic as any he has created. It's also, according to the composer himself, one of the longest: Williams recorded 138 minutes of music with the orchestra—"something of a record," he says.

Looking back on his long experience with the franchise and how it has shaped his career, Williams recalls "the earliest days of *Star Wars* where we introduced the London Symphony Orchestra to the process, which was the first in my experience having an organized orchestra performing a soundtrack, and how wonderful an experience that was."

Pondering what makes his music for *Star Wars* so distinctive, Williams recalls joking with *The Last Jedi* writer/director Rian Johnson about how the beauty of *Star Wars* is that "it's not a science-fiction film, it's a musical," Williams says with a laugh. "So when you go into the mixing, please remember that *Star Wars* will allow us to play music all the time, and basically we do. The orchestra starts with a trumpet blast, and it sort of ends with a trumpet blast, and everything in between has been scored. We don't want to do that with every film, certainly, but the fun of *Star Wars* from a musical point of view is that it's completely sympathetic with music."

For Williams, and for the orchestra, the last day of recording on a film is always emotional, and *The Last Jedi* was no different. "We've been together for so many years," says the composer. "We've finished a lot of films together, so there's always a sense of satisfaction in coming to the end of the musical journey of it. But there's also the sense of feeling sorry that we won't be meeting again next week to record some more *Star Wars* music. We have to look forward to the next episode."

And as for his own long association with *Star Wars*, Williams states: "It's been quite a privilege for a musician to be associated with *Star Wars*. I'm eternally grateful to George Lucas. We all need to be."

2 /

MUSICAL CHARACTERS

An important aspect of John Williams' score for *The Last Jedi*—as it has been for every *Star Wars* film he's scored—is how each character has their own music theme, whether it be Rey, Kylo Ren, Finn, or Rose Tico. "These thematic elements infuse the whole score and are part of what moves the film along, giving it its sonic outline. In the *Star Wars* films, the orchestra can be as extrovert as it wants to be at given times, so it really becomes a big part of the fun and imagination of it all."

Noting that "*The Last Jedi* in particular is rife with interrelationships with characters that we know," Williams enthuses about musically portraying Rey, Finn, Poe Dameron and the other returning characters, as well as new characters like Rose. He also reveals there are some sly nods to the past in the score… "I won't give them away, but there are a couple of really fun inside jokes about how we've disguised some old music that Rian wanted to place here and there. I'll leave the viewers to discover it—or ignore it if they wish—but we had a playful time with it as well."

3 /

1 / *The Last Jedi* boasts a mix of old and new characters, all given distinctive themes by John Williams. (See previous page)

2 / The heroic rogue, Poe Dameron.

3 / Rey (and friend) has an especially inspiring theme.

4 / Luke Skywalker, a character that, like Williams, has been there from the start. (See opposite page)

A LAST(ING) MEMORY

For *The Last Jedi* producer Ram Bergman, getting to witness John Williams at work with the orchestra was a pleasure and a privilege. Stating that he was "wowed" by the experience, Bergman says: "When you are there and you listen to John Williams recording and playing with this 100-piece orchestra, that is the moment you know you are working on a *Star Wars* movie. It was a highlight and one of the best *Star Wars* memories I'll take with me."

ART
FROM A THOUSAND WORLDS

Presenting a gallery of stunning concept art.

1 / The last line of defense. The Resistance take to the trenches on Crait. Art by Kevin Jenkins.

2 /

2 / The First Order scores a direct hit on the hangar bay as Poe and BB-8 are knocked back! Art by Kevin Jenkins.

3 /

4 /

5 /

3 / Luke, Chewie, and Rey keep warm on a cold Ahch-To night. Art by James Carson and Rick Heinrichs.

4 / The well-to-do visitors to Canto Bight mingle. Art by Mauro Borelli and Aaron McBride.

5 / Luke looks on as Rey meditates. Art by Justin Sweet.

6 / No friend of BB-8: Meet BB-9E! Art by Jake Lunt Davies. (See opposite page)

7 /

7 / The Resistance pilots race to engage the enemy in their V-4X-D ski speeders. Art by Kevin Jenkins

8 /

8 / Rey makes the long journey up the steps at Ahch-To.
Art by Kevin Jenkins and James Carson

9 /

9 / Resistance bombers prepare to drop their payloads.
Art by James Clyne

THE POSTERS OF *THE LAST JEDI*

A global hit with audiences around the world, here is a look at some of the stunning poster art that helped build audience anticipation for the movie.

The Dolby Cinema poster illustrated by Paul Shipper

A bold poster variant heralding *The Last Jedi*'s engagement at IMAX theaters.

The Chinese poster for the film.

STAR
THE LAST JEDI
WARS

IN CINEMAS SOON

IN 3D, REAL D 3D AND IMAX 3D

Rey: The distinctive character poster campaign first unveiled at the Official Disney Fan Club event, D23.

STAR
THE LAST JEDI
WARS

IN CINEMAS SOON

IN 3D, REAL D 3D AND IMAX® 3D

Kylo Ren

STAR WARS
THE LAST JEDI

IN CINEMAS SOON

IN 3D, REAL D 3D AND IMAX 3D

Luke Skywalker

STAR
THE LAST JEDI
WARS

IN CINEMAS SOON

IN 3D, REAL D 3D AND IMAX® 3D

General Organa

STAR
THE LAST JEDI
WARS

IN CINEMAS SOON

IN 3D, REAL D 3D AND IMAX 3D

Finn

STAR
THE LAST JEDI
WARS

IN CINEMAS SOON

IN 3D, REAL D 3D AND IMAX® 3D

Poe Dameron

The enigmatic teaser poster

The U.S. release poster

A striking quad poster variant

JEDI
R 15

OTHER GREAT TIE-IN EDITIONS FROM TITAN
ON SALE NOW!

Rogue One: A Star Wars Story
The Official Collector's Edition
ISBN 9781785861574

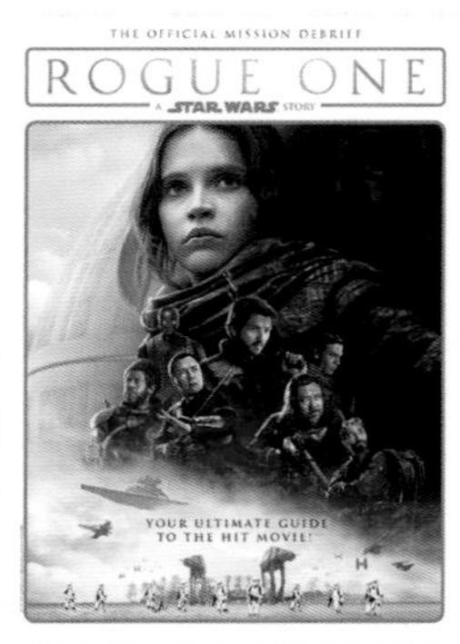

Rogue One: A Star Wars Story
The Official Mission Debrief
ISBN 9781785861581

Star Wars: The Last Jedi
The Official Collector's Edition
ISBN 9781785862113

Star Wars: The Last Jedi
The Official Movie Companion
ISBN 9781785863004

Star Wars:
Lords of the Sith
ISBN 9781785851919

Star Wars:
Heroes of the Force
ISBN 9781785851926

Star Wars:
Icons Of The Galaxy
ISBN 9781785851933

The Best of Star Wars
Insider Volume 1
ISBN 9781785851162

The Best of Star Wars
Insider Volume 2
ISBN 9781785851179

The Best of Star Wars
Insider Volume 3
ISBN 9781785851896

The Best of Star Wars
Insider Volume 4
ISBN 9781785851902

Thor: Ragnarok
The Official Movie Special
ISBN 9781785851179

Black Panther
The Official Movie Special
ISBN 9781785866531

Avengers: Infinity War
The Official Movie Special
ISBN 9781785868054

Ant-Man and the Wasp
The Official Movie Special
ISBN 9781785868092

TITANCOMICS

For more information visit www.titan-comics.com